'Ye shall not eat of any thing that dieth of itself.' We remain faithful to this interdict of Deuteronomy and kill the animals we consume. We do not permit just any manner of slaughter, yet it is necessary to spill blood in order to transform a body into something edible, into meat we are prepared to buy from the butcher.

Nevertheless, we do not want to witness this slaughter. We no longer tolerate sacrifices, publicing butchering during festivals, butchers operating openly in the middle of our cities. Today, animals are killed in invisible abattoirs, set a good distance from our normal activities. This recent separation between the slaughterhouse and the butcher's establishment is somehow essential to the modern meat diet. Why do we find it necessary to slaughter living animals in order to enjoy their flesh? And why does this act offend our sensibilities, without necessarily making us into vegetarians? In her study of abattoirs in south-west France, Noëlie Vialles brings to light a complex system of avoidances. Her analysis reveals that beyond the specific denial of the work of the abattoirs lies a whole system of symbolic representations of blood, human beings and animals, a symbolic code that determines the way in which we prepare domestic animals for the table.

Cet ouvrage est publié dans le cadre de l'accord de co-édition passé en 1977 entre la Fondation de la Maison des Sciences de l'Homme et le Press Syndicate of the University of Cambridge. Toutes les langues européennes sont admises pour les titres couverts par cet accord, et les ouvrages collectifs peuvent paraître en plusieurs langues.

Les ouvrages paraissent soit isolément, soit dans l'une des séries que la Maison des Sciences de l'Homme et Cambridge University Press ont convenu de publier ensemble. La distribution dans le monde entier des titres ainsi publiés conjointement par les deux établissements est assurée par Cambridge University Press.

This book is published as part of the joint publishing agreement established in 1977 between the Fondation de la Maison des Sciences de l'Homme and the Press Syndicate of the University of Cambridge. Titles published under this arrangement may appear in any European language or, in the case of volumes of collected essays, in several languages.

New books will appear either as individual titles or in one of the series which the Maison des Sciences de l'Homme and Cambridge University Press have jointly agreed to publish. All books published jointly by the Maison des Sciences de l'Homme and Cambridge University Press will be distributed by the Press throughout the world.

ANIMAL TO EDIBLE

Published by the Press Syndicate of the University of Cambridge
The Pitt Building, Trumpington Street, Cambridge CB2 1RP
40 West 20th Street, New York, NY 10011–4211, USA
10 Stamford Road, Oakleigh, Melbourne 3166, Australia

Originally published in French as *Le sang et la chair: les abattoirs des pays de l'Adour*
by Fondation de la Maison des Sciences de l'Homme

First published in English by Cambridge University Press 1994
as *Animal to edible*

A catalogue record for this book is available from the British Library

Library of Congress cataloguing in publication data

Vialles, Noëlle.
[Sang et la chair. English]
Blood and flesh : the abattoirs of South-West France / Noëlle Vialles : translated
from the French by J. A. Underwood.
p. cm.
Includes bibliographical references (p.) and index.
ISBN 0–521–44098–X (hc)
1. Slaughtering and slaughter-houses – France – History.
I. Title.
TS1966.F7V5313 1994
664'.9029'0944–dc20 93–32138 CIP

ISBN 0 521 44098 X hardback
ISBN 0 521 466725 paperback
ISBN 2 7351 0573 3 hardback (France only)
ISBN 2 73512 0574 1 paperback (France only)

Transferred to digital printing 2002

Funding for the English translation of this book was made available through a grant from the French Ministry of Culture and Francophony.

CE

CONTENTS

LIST OF ILLUSTRATIONS AND INSETS

Illustrations

Insets

PREFACE

This is a remarkable book in several ways. The subject is a most unusual one (an anthropological study of the abattoirs of the Adour region of south-west France); the writing exhibits considerable refinement and precision; and the author's analyses are richly abundant. Certainly it will surprise no one to learn that Noëlie Vialles's study, funded by the Ethnological Heritage Department in the context of an invitation for bids on the theme of 'popular naturalist knowledge', is the only one of its kind. We have had historical works concerning the butcher's trade in different periods, highly specialised veterinary texts, essays, novels, even films about the slaughter of animals. But never before have we had an ethnological analysis based on the physical presence of the observer, on patient analysis of locations and actions, and on attentive listening to the comments of those involved in this immense daily drama.

The first thing Noëlie Vialles had to do was to gain the confidence of abattoir personnel, from cattlemen to secretaries. In particular she had to gain the confidence of the people in whose persons and actions is concentrated the essence of the imaginative world surrounding the killing of animals, namely the slaughtermen, the *abatteurs* who used to be called *tueurs* [literally, 'killers'],* and that meant, in the first place, overcoming deep incomprehension as well as doubts as to the ethnologist's true intentions ('But there's nothing to see here').

The fact is, the initial question is itself a difficult one to hear. This is because we all (slaughtermen included) operate on the basis of what to us are self-evident facts. We never question them: indeed, they give every appearance of being natural phenomena that there is no need for us to understand. What is 'meat', in fact? What do people mean when they talk about 'true meat', or butcher's meat, that supreme food? The veterinary definition ('edible product of animal origin') is clearly inadequate, for we can be sure that it implicitly

* *Translator's note*: This study being largely concerned with the (sometimes changing) use of language in the context of the slaughterhouse, it will not always be appropriate to seek to translate (into a language that has itself borrowed the word 'abattoir') the key terms involved. Where it would seem useful, an English gloss (or the original French) will be supplied in square brackets.

excludes eggs, milk, fish, and shellfish – all products that nevertheless meet the definition. Moreover, we all know and indeed take for granted that not all animal flesh is edible, that the flesh of certain animals cannot be termed meat, and finally that meat exists only after an animal has been deliberately put to death, and that means bled to death. In short, Noëlie Vialles raises a disturbing question: how are we to understand the operation (a kind of 'ellipsis between animal and meat') that turns an animal into something edible rather than a repulsive corpse?

That ellipsis, that major area of obscurity, is something that modern standards of slaughtering draw out indefinitely and highlight to a very much greater degree than was the case in the old days, when slaughtering was performed in the familiar surroundings of the street. A series of dissociations, linked in an ever finer chain, surrounds (and at the same time evades) the crucial moment of the kill. There is first of all, within a space that is wholly directional and in which the route is irreversible ('fatal', indeed), the separation of the abattoir into 'dirty sector' (the living, moistly warm biological realm) and 'clean sector' (bloodless, refrigerated). Between the two is the 'slaughterhall', where a whole series of operations succeed one another: immobilisation, stunning, hanging, bleeding, flaying, evisceration, splitting, and weighing. The crucial operation is bleeding, which is kept entirely separate from the others. A staggered layout ensures that the men in the slaughterhall and the animals entering cannot see one another. Immobilised in the 'trap' [usually referred to as the 'stunning pen' in an English abattoir, but for reasons that will become apparent in chapter 5, a literal translation of the French term '*piège*' is used here], the animal is first stunned. It is then swung round through a right angle, hoisted up (it will never touch the ground again), and bled. The separation of the two operations (performed by different operators) not only introduces an element of doubt as to the identity of the death-dealing action; it also blurs the actual moment of death. Two men do the killing, yet neither really kills. The first administers an anaesthetic; the second merely bleeds an inert animal. No one can say at what point that animal ceased to be alive.

All these major disjunctive actions, at the end of which a meat-bearing carcass has been extracted from the live animal, reach beyond the profit-related mechanisation of the operations involved (through fragmenting the job into its component parts) to recreate the symbolic dimension behind the occupational and hygiene standards observed and imposed. Unbeknown to the legislator, they reconstruct a world of symbols that dies hard. I leave it to the reader to assess the complexity of the field once the author has finished presenting her dispassionate, detailed, and scholarly analyses of it.

I should like, if I may, to indulge in just a couple of variations on one of the aspects outlined in the following pages, namely that of the vegetalising metaphor. 'The substance meat is something organic obtained by dislocating the biological' and by replacing the animal with a human creation, as signified by the expression *faire la bête* [literally, 'doing/making the animal'; see below, p. 56]. This covers the sum total of the operations that turn the animal that walked into the building into the weighed, suspended carcass that goes out. However, in the detail of the operations that 'make' an animal there can be seen, beneath the current terminology, a series of associations closely linking the animal and vegetable kingdoms. It is a question, one might almost say, of aligning the animal (in the special form represented by cattle) on the tree, of 'gathering' meat as one gathers a vegetable, almost of reducing the carnivorous aspect of human eating to its vegetarian aspect. We are all familiar with meat being displayed on the butcher's slab surrounded by greenery (even if nowadays the greenery is usually of a synthetic kind), but here it is the words themselves that interest us because they say what there is to be said. Take *abattage*, for example, a bringing down of something that was standing, euphemistically applied to the felling of trees as well as to the slaughter of animals, or *habillage*, a curious technical term [dressing] considering that here it has more to do with undressing (it refers to a process that begins with the removal of the animal's skin) but one that makes sense with reference to the vocabulary of the woodcutter (for whom *abillier* is the technical term describing the preparation of a stripped billet of firewood). But the most interesting word of all, which describes a fast-disappearing practice, is *fleurer* (also *faire des fleurs* ['doing flowers']). This refers to an operation performed during the flaying of large animals, when a knife is used to make regular, contrasting incisions in the flesh suggestive of 'the raked sand of a Zen garden'. Possibly the reference is to the skilled knifework involved in lightly grazing [*effleurer*] the animal *à fleur de peau* ['skin-deep'], or perhaps it merely denotes the aesthetic design inscribed on the flesh that is thus de-animalised. In either case, to my mind the expressions once again evoke the vegetable kingdom (the *Littré* dictionary gives *fleuri* ['bloom'] as 'the subtly shaded appearance presented by certain logs after being sawn').

It seems to me that we ought perhaps to see in this kind of persistence of symbols a very ancient heritage that comes down to us from the Bible. In the beginning, the Garden of Eden was vegetarian. Men and animals ate only plant food. It was only in a second era, following the Flood, that God decided to let men eat the flesh of animals. However, such meat must be bloodless (the sacrificial blood was God's alone) and it must be taken only from vegetarian animals, the prototype being the ruminant. In this way meat may be seen as the ultimate transmutation of vegetable matter (grass), once an animal has lost at man's hand what distinguishes it from the plants that fed it, namely warm blood and mobility – a necessary effusion if we accept the correlations that exist between the different bodily secretions and consequently between blood and the physical aspects of sexuality, which no one would dream of saying belonged to the vegetable kingdom. In a way, de-animated, de-animalised, and even de-sexualised, butcher's 'meat' can no longer be anything but the quintessence of the vegetable.

Françoise Héritier-Augé
March 1987

Outside the town . . .

But there are special places outside the town where all blood and dirt are first washed off in running water. The slaughtering of livestock and cleaning of carcasses is done by slaves [condemned criminals sentenced to hard labour]. *They don't let ordinary people get used to cutting up animals, because they think it tends to destroy one's natural feelings of humanity. It's also forbidden to bring anything dirty or unhygienic inside the town, for fear of polluting the atmosphere and so causing disease.*

Sir Thomas More, *Utopia* (1516), ii.2

INTRODUCTION

Abattoirs may seem an odd and, to many people, slightly disturbing subject to be interested in, given the bloody images they conjure up and the repugnant sensory impressions they arouse. Even those who work in them do not hide their surprise at being the focus of attention for no obvious professional reason. Why not choose a less repellent field of study? This at least indicates how far the representations of which they know themselves to be the object are internalised – to the extent, in fact, of implicitly reflecting them back on the intruder, who is then almost suspected of having dubious motives (why this desire to become acquainted with things that everyone 'normally', in the absence of some compelling obligation, prefers not to know about?).

Ethnologists themselves not infrequently react in much the same way, though their concern is at a purely professional level. Where, they wonder, is the pleasure to be had in such a study, the implication being that without some pleasurable experience ethnological fieldwork is mostly drudgery and tedium?

If what is meant is that abattoirs are hardly likely to delight the senses, no one will disagree (certainly not anyone who is familiar with such places). If what is meant is that the sort of people found there, notably slaughterers, could not possibly provide rewarding company, this can only be seen as an example of the common prejudice regarding such people. However, one of the ethnologist's professional obligations is to overcome every kind of prejudice and not exclude a single human being from the human race, which is his/her field of study. *Nihil humanum* ...

Finally, if by pleasure is meant the satisfaction of learning and seeking to understand, what is really being asked is this: what intellectual motivation, what concrete question directed attention towards this particular field of activity? Quite simply, it is this: what is meat?

What is meat?

The question may appear pointless, even slightly naive. In our somewhat overfed societies, meat is a familiar reality, found on our tables, in our kitchens, even on the street (in the butcher's shop window). We distinguish various kinds of meat, indicating preferences for one or another. We speak of 'red', 'white', or 'dark' meats, light or fortifying meats, healthy or heavy meats, and so on. We attribute various qualities to them; above all it is 'butcher's meat' that we think of as 'true meat'. But what is 'butcher's meat' exactly? Does pork count as butcher's meat, or is it the province of the *charcutier* [as the French pork butcher is called]? Or take goat, which is marketed by poulterers: does that count as butcher's meat? And what of poultry, rabbits, game? Even the most superficial glance would suggest that we distinguish 'infra' and 'ultra' meats. Possibly 'true meat' (e.g., Méchin 1983, p. 98; see below, References, pp. 135 ff.) is in fact a norm. At least, it is not something that is immediately obvious.

We know that for a very long time *viande* [the French word for 'meat'] meant all types of food, not just animal flesh as food. Think of the Italian *vivanda*, which has the same root. Until the eighteenth century the expression 'Lenten meat' [*viande de carême*] was used to refer to fish. In the same way as *viande* eventually came to signify animal flesh as food, the Greek word *opson* usually meant sardine or anchovy. To the point where 'fish' in modern Greek is *psari*, a derivative of *opson*. The development of vocabulary often provides a very clear indication of the way in which a society's eating habits evolved (Revel 1979, p. 82).

Bloch and Wartburg's 'Etymological Dictionary of the French Language' gives under '*viande*':

until the seventeenth century, denotes any type of food; ... specialised in the modern sense from the seventeenth century onwards ... Latin *vivenda*, 'that which is used for life', derived from *vivere*, 'to live' (Bloch and Wartburg 1932, Vol. II, p. 367).

As we see, meat is what sustains life, so it is understandable that, even while the meaning narrowed down, it retained the initial connotation of a very exalted type of food. But what is 'animal flesh as food', exactly? What is the 'modern sense' of the word?

Asked this question, a wide variety of respondents supplied answers that are summed up pretty well in the technical wording of one vet's definition: meat is 'an edible product of animal origin'. And eggs, milk? Fish, molluscs, crustaceans? 'Naturally', these are excluded, but implicitly, because this is something that 'goes by itself'. It goes *without saying* that not all animals' flesh can be eaten, that the flesh of certain animals is not meat, and that meat is obtained only by slaughter. In addition to these implicit assumptions there are various customs. For instance, some birds are regarded not as meat but as fish. This was so of puffins in England, at least in medieval times (Jackson, in Kuper 1981, p. 47, n. 1; Lister 1986, p. 43); it was also true in France (and still is, by many accounts) of birds that live in an aquatic environment and eat mainly fish. Habitat and feeding habits are thus more important than species as regards defining the human culinary category in which an animal is placed.

We are familiar with the provisions that Moses laid down regarding permitted animals and how they were to be killed and cooked, and we know of his ban on consuming their blood. We also know that these ritual standards, in dedicating the children of Israel to 'purity' (in other words to separation from their 'idolatrous' neighbours), formed part of an organised world view. Christianity very soon abandoned these arrangements, announcing particularly through St Paul that 'everything that God created is good, and nothing is to be rejected when it is taken with thanksgiving' (I Timothy 4:4; NEB); nevertheless, for economic reasons Christian teaching was to retain the ban on blood and 'anything that has been strangled' (e.g., Acts 15:20) for a time, and from the seventh century onwards it several times prohibited the eating of horseflesh (Lizet 1982). So we are not, apparently, in thrall to any strict, normative eating code. However, we are undoubtedly heirs to a particular cultural history (in which the Christian influence is not the only one), since we do conform to rules in the matter of food, particularly meat. We do not regard the flesh of all animals as food, we eat very little blood, with the notable exception of pig's blood, and we reject 'dead meats' and 'anything that has been strangled' (except for the famous *canard au sang*, though this has not necessarily been strangled; see Pomiane [1924] 1952, p. 279).

Finally, and perhaps most importantly, meat is obtained only by slaughtering animals. Animals that have died a natural death or have died as the result of illness or accident are thought of as being unfit to eat. So there has to be slaughter. Not every sort of slaughter produces meat, though: the animal's blood must be shed. On these two points the provisions of the Mosaic law and the regulations governing abattoirs are in full agreement.

Yet slaughter, whether ritual or regulation, is still not sufficient to obtain meat. A further requisite is that it be applied to a permitted species. If a cat were killed like a rabbit and popped in the pot, we should still find it shocking and far from appetising, because cat is 'not eaten'. It was the presumption and sometimes the certainty of this kind of practice (and many others even more dreadful) that accounted for the poor reputation of the old 'pieman' (Sébillot 1981, pp. 68–71).

However, this killing is something we would rather know nothing about. In former times, sacrifices were solemn occasions celebrated in public. Later, slaughterhouses operated in the middle of towns, when animals were not actually killed in the street. Nowadays, slaughtering has become an invisible, exiled, almost clandestine activity. We know it goes on, of course, but it is an abstract kind of knowledge. We have no wish to eat corpses (we are carnivores, not carrion-eaters), so animals have to be slaughtered. But we demand an ellipsis between animal and meat. Advertisers are well aware of this and take scrupulous account of it; they need, for example, to be very careful how they vaunt the 'flavour' of French lamb or the 'punch' packed by beef. 'Ancestral taboos' about blood, which in the Middle Ages put butchers in the same category as executioners, barbers, and surgeons (Le Goff 1977, p. 93), still live on today, accounting for our confusion in the presence of men whose principal occupation is to slaughter animals: '*In reality* the butcher does not kill, he works; but *in truth* he kills, and therein lies the whole mystery' (Legendre 1978, p. 856).

Certainly the butcher enjoys a quieter image nowadays. He is no longer witnessed killing animals; in fact it has become unusual for him to practise slaughtering himself. Private slaughtering is now illegal, and it has become possible for us to be unaware that the skilled hand we see trimming the meat was the instrument of the animal's death. 'Dispensed from himself doing the slaughtering, the urban butcher is henceforth required only to handle an anonymous flesh reduced to its cold materiality', writes Pierre Gascar (Gascar 1973, p. 105), who goes on to analyse the benefit that we draw from this 'dispensation':

> The individuality and physical outline of the animal, abruptly reinforced in the brief death struggle, is replaced through the butcher's art by countless quarters, cuts, joints, and pieces of offal that have been familiar to us in shape and appearance for long enough to have acquired a certain autonomy in our eyes, a reality independent of the whole in which they were once comprised ... No more bullock, no more death. The butcher's shop has become a place of innocence. (*ibid*., p. 124)

However, that 'innocence' results only from having transferred to other people the mark of blood of which today's butcher has virtually been washed clean. Who those other people are we simply do not wish to know; the mere thought of their existence somehow gives us the shivers. We are paradoxical carnivores, deeming suspect a job that has to be done. How, we wonder, could anyone be a slaughterer?

Granted, this is not the only case in which conflicting demands come together in this way. Nearly all the circumstances in which we look for the 'clean' lead us to reject, along with the 'dirty', the people who get rid of dirt for us. Even the preoccupation with cleanliness, once it leads us to look more closely into ways of providing it, seems slightly unhealthy, as witness Parent-Duchâtelet's astonishing contemporary account of prostitution in early nineteenth-century Paris (Parent-Duchâtelet [1836] 1981).

Our rejection of the 'dirty' is the more vigorous, the more closely it threatens us and the more viscerally it affects us. Thus everything to do with death, be it that of men or of animals, is kept firmly in the background, even when we set great store by the end achieved thereby. 'The whitening instinct of white Anglo–Saxon America' is not sufficient to engender a frank acceptance of the 'morticians' who nevertheless flourish there; the fact that pathologists contribute towards medical progress does not make us any the less mistrustful of them; in fact one of their number has said that, for members of such professions, 'an honest answer to the question of what one does for a living has every chance of spoiling the party in no time' (Gonzalez-Crussi 1984).

Similarly, it has been suggested that the most ardent advocates of the death penalty would be loath to invite to dinner the man whom French, with steadfast euphemism, calls an *exécuteur des hautes oeuvres* (Delarue 1979, p. 30). In exactly the same way, our massive consumption of meat and meat products does nothing to warm our hearts towards those who slaughter the animals concerned.

We thus make a threefold distinction: in terms of our demands, in terms of the realities, and between people. We want the obverse of the coin but without the reverse. So what do they do, the people who are directly confronted on the reverse? That is to say, what do we do when (what would we do if) forced to face up to this alimentary murder?

If we stick to the reassuring (yet at the same time disturbing) prejudice that makes us think of those who perform these essential tasks as being somehow different, we do indeed gain by keeping them at a distance from our 'normality', attributing their acceptance of such activity to some kind of deviance, some socially useful but psychologically perverted pathology. However, even if there were some truth in this hypothesis, it would not be enough to let us completely off the hook. The negative choices made by a culture are as significant as its positive choices, and the same impulse leads it to deliver models of good behaviour as to deliver models of shocking behaviour (Devereux [1970] 1977, ch. 8). We must therefore reject this convenient dichotomy in order to examine how our culture proceeds when brought face to face with the death of animals, since neither is vegetarianism prevalent in it, nor do the vegetarians contrive at best to do more than stir our sensibilities without significantly altering what we do.

With this, a close study of slaughtering takes on an anthropological dimension.

Theoretical demarcation

Nothing in the question underlying this study dictated the choice of the Adour region; that was prompted simply by reasons of convenience as regarded carrying out the relevant fieldwork. The geographical boundary coincides more or less with administrative boundaries, taking in the four *départements* of Pyrénées-Atlantiques, Hautes-Pyrénées, Gers, and Landes. There is no strictly ethnological relevance in this grouping, but nor is there anything wildly inappropriate. If our aim is to perceive a regional unity as well as local variations, the choice of territory allows us to do this, offering as it does both the overall homogeneity of a reduced 'South West' (the Garonne valley being excluded) and the internal diversity guaranteed by the different ethnic regions of Gascony, Béarn, and the Basque Country.

Nevertheless, the conceptual demarcation is the more important one, being directly bound up with the question behind the study. Granted, the same question could equally well have led to a study of hunting, fishing, the domestic killing of pigs or poultry, or the industrial slaughter of the same. But apart from the fact that entering any field involves making an opening somewhere (and the further fact that certain aspects of the potential field have been covered quite thoroughly already), the slaughter of large livestock is not only less familiar but lies at the very heart of the problem of 'butcher's meat' or 'true meat'.

Even defined this narrowly, the relevant field of activity presents major variations with regard to volume, plant, and consequently methods used. Some abattoirs are genuinely industrial, others still operate very much on an artisan scale. Accordingly, the people who work in them neither enjoy the same working conditions, nor possess the same skills, nor have the same training behind them. Yet everywhere the same decisive transformation is effected.

Right from the initial contact, it became clear that this already restricted delimitation was going to be reduced still further. The fact is that although, seen from outside, the study of abattoirs, of slaughtering, and hence of slaughtermen would seem to amount to much the same thing, this is far from being the case.

A number of activities come together on the premises of an abattoir or slaughterhouse [the words are interchangeable in English usage]:

Animals enter the premises alive and leave in the form of carcasses. 'Buying live and selling dead' is the definition of the work of the wholesale butcher. This involves the provision of refrigerated storage rooms and sometimes cutting rooms as well, to which must be added the personnel responsible for transporting the animals on the one hand and the meat on the other. Some retail butchers do their own buying and transporting to the abattoir of the animals they have arranged to have slaughtered there. Lastly, private individuals also bring animals to be slaughtered for their own domestic consumption (this applies particularly to calves and pigs, which are then stored in freezers or in accordance with traditional methods).

The animals may spend several hours in waiting pens [collectively called lairage, in English] before being slaughtered. The upkeep of the pens and the care of the animals are the responsibility of cattlemen.

Animals and carcasses are subject to hygiene controls, which are provided by a staff of vets and inspectors.

The abattoir as workplace has its own personnel providing constant maintenance and cleaning services.

By-products are treated or stored before being removed from the premises, so there are also tripe-dressing rooms, gut rooms, and places for the curing of hides, together with the requisite personnel.

An abattoir produces waste. The liquid effluent usually undergoes initial treatment on site before being dispatched to municipal purification plants or straight into a sewage main. Solid waste on the other hand is regularly removed in tankers and taken away to rendering establishments, of which there are very few: some 90 per cent of the waste from the abattoirs of these four *départements* is taken away and treated by a single Agen company.

Very occasionally (in two abattoirs only) blood is collected, in which case bleeding is done by trocar (see figures 28–31, and below, pp. 84–5). Chilled and subsequently congealed, the blood is sold to manufacturers of pharmaceutical products. The process requires few staff (one or two persons) but suitable premises and equipment.

Almost invariably in the case of public abattoirs a caretaker or manager will have accommodation on the premises in order to provide a round-the-clock emergency slaughtering service. Where this is not the case, everyone knows who should be contacted in an emergency, at least through the local vets.

Finally, whether the abattoir is private or public, its activities are organised and controlled by managers, administrators, and an accounts department, assisted in the case of the larger abattoirs by a secretariat.

Without losing sight of these many activities, the present study will concentrate on the work of slaughterers, since it is this that constitutes the core of our problem.

Concrete diversity

In the four *départements* under consideration, abattoirs in both the private and public sectors are distributed as follows:

1. *Number of abattoirs*

département	public	private	total
Pyrénées-Atlantiques	8	2	10
Hautes-Pyrénées	6	0	6
Landes	5	0	5
Gers	8	3	11
total	27	5	32

The map reproduced as figure 3 shows their geographical distribution.

Volumes of activity vary enormously, from 100 tonnes [metric tons] a year to more than 12,000. Figure 2 takes no account of private abattoirs, which do not always issue precise figures. This much can be said, however: one private abattoir in Gers *département* slaughters approximately 10,000 tonnes a year, while the rest, which specialise in slaughtering pigs, seem appreciably smaller. Here we confine ourselves to round-number quantities gathered *in situ*. We were able to consult the studies available to departmental veterinary services; however, except in Landes *département*, recent changes that in some cases substantially altered the quantities dealt with by abattoirs have not yet been taken into account in the periodic evaluations. The closure of some of the very small abattoirs, major technical improvements, spectacular modernisations of dilapidated premises, and the arrival or departure of the clientele of a wholesaler-shipper are among the changes that can very quickly modify quantities slaughtered.

2. *Distribution of tonnages (in metric tons)*

annual tonnages	Pyrénées-Atlantiques	Hautes-Pyrénées	Landes	Gers	total no. of abattoirs	total tonnages
≡ 12,000	2				2	23,000
≡ 8,000				2	2	16,000
5,500–4,000	1	1	1		3	14,500
3,500–3,000		1	1	1	3	9,700
2,800–2,000	2		2	1	5	11,800
1,300–1,200	1	1		1	3	3,800
950–650	1	1		2	4	3,000
400–100	1	2	1	1	5	1,350
tonnage per *dépt.*	35,800	10,120	12,950	24,280	27	83,150

Figure 2 calls for some elaboration:

The four largest abattoirs between them handle nearly half the tonnage slaughtered in the four *départements*. Two of them are in Pyrénées-Atlantique (Pau, Anglet), the other two in Gers (Auch, Miélan). This arrangement suggests a bi-polarisation of slaughtering facilities that coincides more with cattle-rearing areas than with centres of consumption. This is in line with a policy U-turn as regards siting abattoirs. It used to be the case that large abattoirs were built in the vicinity of centres of consumption, until it became clear that it would make just as much sense to put them near areas of production, the reason being that transporting meat in refrigerator vans tends to pose fewer practical problems than transporting live cattle. Nationally, for example, very large abattoirs have been set up in the key cattle-rearing areas of Poitou-Charentes, Charolais, and Lyonnais. On a smaller scale, the same type of distribution can be seen here.

The mean national tonnage (total tonnage divided by number of abattoirs) is between 4,000 and 5,000 tonnes a year. As figure 2 shows, this volume is achieved by only three of our abattoirs, almost two-thirds of which handle fewer than 2,800 tonnes a year. Probably at least half of these small abattoirs are destined to disappear as part of a modernisation policy that has been in hand for over twenty years and that aims to reduce the number of abattoirs while increasing their size. Meanwhile, until the policy has been fully implemented, as figure 2 indicates the mean volume of the region's abattoirs (approximately 3,080 tonnes a year) is not in itself significant in that seventeen abattoirs out of twenty-seven have a capacity well below that average.

It goes without saying that such disparities in abattoir capacity mean enormous variations in the equipment at their disposal, in the working conditions and levels of skill of the slaughtermen, and in the spirit and atmosphere of the workplace.

These disparities affect the rhythm of work. If the larger abattoirs are able to keep up an hourly rate of 25–30 large bovines, 90–100 calves, 80–100 pigs, 120–140 sheep, and 350–400 lambs, it is impossible to assess hourly rates for an abattoir handling fewer than 2,800 metric tons a year.

Finally, the number of slaughterers (as of staff in general) depends on the capacity of the abattoir and may vary between thirty and two. They are nearly all men. Women are found in tripe-dressing rooms, in hygiene control, and of course in the offices, but I came across only two women currently employed on a slaughter line, and even they were assigned to dehairing and 'finishing' pig carcasses.

The status of slaughterers also varies greatly. Four main categories are distinguishable:

municipal contract slaughterers,
employees of craftsman slaughterers, wholesale butchers, or private firms,
craftsmen working alone or, more usually, with a small team of employees,
and lastly butchers who do their own slaughtering of the meat they sell; like the craftsmen slaughterers, they usually employ their own teams.

These status differences find very clear expression in relations among the men or between them and the various authorities (management, hygiene inspectors, wholesale butchers), so much so, in fact, that one glance into a slaughterhall was almost sufficient to determine the status of every occupant.

Work invariably began very early, around 6 a.m. but sometimes as early as 4 a.m. Probably this should be seen as a survival of old habits (in the days before refrigeration, the preparation of meat was done during the coolest hours of the day. Sometimes the other end of the day was used and butchers demanded late work, keeping slaughterers on the job until far into the night.

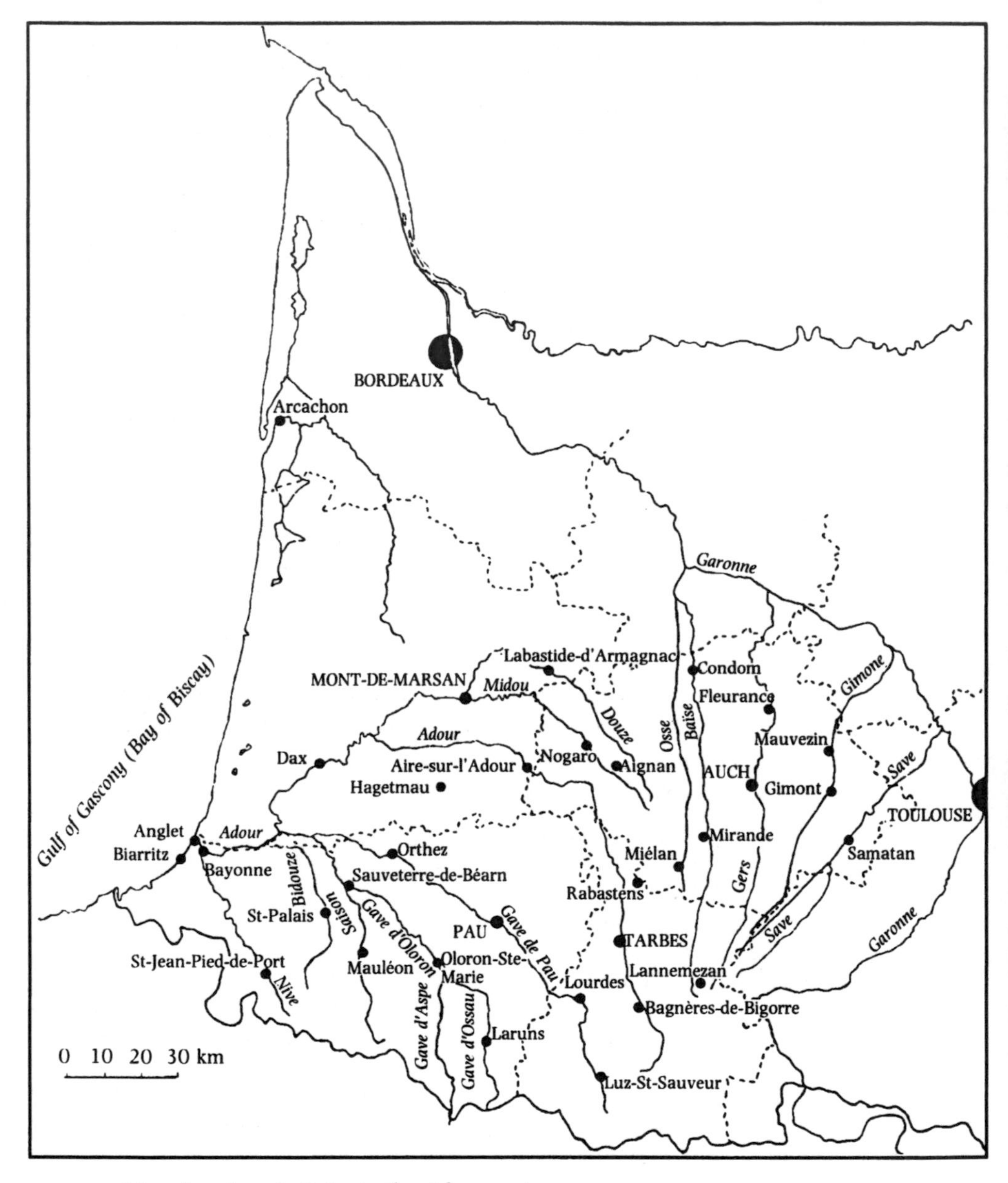

3 Map showing abattoirs in the Adour region

That no longer happens, and work usually stops around 2 or 4 p.m. Knocking-off time fluctuates, in fact, according to the days of the week and the seasons of the year. The busiest days are usually Monday and Thursday or Friday; the busiest times of year are more variable, depending on the species being slaughtered (notably calves and sheep) and the quantities to be dealt with. All other things being equal, in a tourist region, for example, slaughtering will see a busy period in the summer.

The organisation of slaughtering depends on the premises and plant available and may differ widely from one establishment to another. Generally speaking, however, pigs are slaughtered in a part of the premises more or less clearly separated from the other slaughter lines and at the beginning of the day. The slaughter of large bovines or calves goes on at the same time, and finally it is the turn of the ovines [sheep]. This order may be changed, however, particularly if a very much larger quantity of one species is to be slaughtered than of other species, in which case that species will tend to be dealt with first.

However the work is organised, there is a break around 8 or 10 a.m. during which the slaughterers have something to eat. Occasionally they may prepare a proper hot meal, but often they must be content with a quick snack.

In every case it was during actual work that contact was most easily made, because the conversation mostly concerned the job itself, and on the job it is possible for a certain skill and with it a certain dignity to become manifest, qualities that are often denied to '*tueurs*' (as they call themselves). The initial contact once established, one could then continue the interview outside working hours, going back over what had been merely alluded to, discussing photographs, and, when projection facilities were available, screening and discussing Georges Franju's vivid short film, *Le sang des bêtes* (1947; released in the UK as 'The Slaughterhouse' in 1949).

Observations and conversations were not equally fruitful and convenient on every site and with every person approached, which is why certain abattoirs and certain interviewees were 'picked out' or rather stood out from the rest. In fact, an initial exploratory tour of the abattoirs of the region under consideration soon revealed that some were exemplary in terms of layout, plant, and operation; it also provided an opportunity for opening relations with certain persons that the subsequent course of the study was devoted to developing. So the present work does not in any way claim to be exhaustive, nor could it possibly be seen as such. All it seeks to do is to use some of the material gathered in an attempt to perceive the essence of the field defined by our leading question: what is meat, specifically 'butcher's meat'?

1

A PLACE THAT IS NO-PLACE

From confusion to dissociation

The definition of *abattoir* that Émile Littré gave in the very first edition of his 'Dictionary of the French language' (1863–72) was reproduced without change in all subsequent editions from 1878 to 1961. Here it is in full:

> Place set aside for the slaughter of animals such as bullocks, calves, sheep, etc. that are used for human consumption. Abattoirs are located outside the surrounding walls of towns.

The abattoir is thus defined in terms of activity and location. The word itself is recent, appearing in 1806 (Bloch and Wartburg 1932) at the same time as Napoleon's major reorganization of slaughtering and butchery.

Before that, butchers used to slaughter animals in the middle of town, sometimes right beside the stall from which the meat was sold. Throughout the Middle Ages and up until the eighteenth century, the 'Grande Boucherie de Paris' flourished in the St-Jacques-la-Boucherie quarter (now Châtelet and Les Halles), close to the fish market, the pillory, and the riverbank square known as the 'place de la Grève', where executions were held, and not far from 'Miracle Court' and the Cemetery of the Holy Innocents. As Pierre Gascar writes:

> The whole grandeur (and horror) of the Middle Ages lies in such associations, in this kind of promiscuity, this mingling; the charnel house of the Holy Innocents with its mud-caked skulls in open-air loggias amid stalls of fruit and meat and fish; hanged criminals in the smell of the tide; religious banners being paraded among tubs of entrails (Gascar 1973, p. 41).

Literary bombast? Mercier, describing the city towards the end of the eighteenth century, was able to write: 'Streets too narrow and poorly laid out, houses that are too tall and stop the air from circulating freely, butchers' shops, fishmongers, sewers, and cemeteries corrupt the atmosphere' (Mercier [1781–8] 1982, p. 39). A new concern for the salubrity of the atmosphere, which Corbin analyses in detail (Corbin 1982)? No doubt, but the description is there. Mercier goes on:

4 *The butchers shop*, Annibale Carracci, c. 1580.
Oil on wood, 59.7 × 71 cm., Kimbell Art Museum, Fort Worth, Texas.

What could be more revolting, more disgusting than to slit animals' throats and cut them up in public? One steps in congealed blood. In some butchers' shops the bullock is led beneath the meat on display. The animal sees it, sniffs, draws back; it is pulled forward, hauled forward, bellowing; dogs nip its ankles as the drovers stun it in order to drag it into the place of death (quoted in Salvetti 1980, p. 29).

There is a wealth of accounts of the kind of spectacle that city streets presented in the Middle Ages and even up until the late eighteenth century. Many historical works have now been written, either devoted entirely to the subject (e.g., Leguay 1984) or touching on it occasionally (Ariès 1977; Chaudieu 1965 and 1980; Corbin 1982; Farge 1979a; Guerrand 1985; Lebigre 1979; Thomas 1983; and many others). Presumably the situation was very similar in the provinces to what it was in towns and much the same in the rest of Europe as it was in France.

Throughout history the work done in shops and booths had spilled out on to the public thoroughfare; when necessary the street formed a convenient extension to the workshop at the same time as providing a sewer. In short, the street was always a place where animals could be seen having their throats cut (Agulhon 1981, p. 85).

On several occasions, as towns increased in size and meat-eating (which we know to have varied enormously from social class to social class) became more widespread, local or national authorities tried to have slaughterhouses (*tueries*, or '*écorcheries* [*écorcher* = to flay]', as they were called up until the early nineteenth century; they are still referred to as *tueries* in the [French] legislation banning private slaughterhouses) removed from towns. However, it was only under the Consulate [1799–1804], and to an even greater extent under the Empire [1804–14], that radical steps were taken in this regard. And the chief of these, the one that seems to me to give the others a coherence and effectiveness that no previous decision had possessed, was the prohibition of private slaughtering coupled with the obligation to have slaughtering performed in municipal establishments built far from urban centres, in other words the *dissociation of slaughtering and butchery*. This was the measure that 'cleared' the butcher and made him 'innocent', the measure that cleaned up the streets and took account of the new sensibilities. But it was also, as we shall see, the measure that transferred the images of death and blood to abattoirs and those who worked in them.

From this time on it was possible for the regulations governing butchery, which had existed at least since the Romans' *suarii*, *boarii*, and *pecuarii*, to be dissociated from those governing slaughtering.

The latter were to have six main areas of concern:

The setting-up of slaughterhouses and their obligations in terms of a 'service in the public interest'.

Standards of hygiene regarding the work and the product (meat). These cover all the jobs involved, including what tools are permitted, what they may be made of (knives with wooden handles are prohibited, for example, wood being capable of carrying germs), the use of water to wash down carcasses (instead of the rags still in use quite recently), the cleanliness of working clothes and of the workers themselves, and so on.

Standards of hygiene regarding animals and meat. These are implemented by veterinary and sanitary-inspection staff. The fact that abattoirs made this kind of control easier was one of the main reasons why they were set up.

'Humane' standards of treatment for animals. These became increasingly rigorous and restrictive (i.e., backed up by sanctions). For example, it was prohibited to suspend an animal, whatever the means employed, before it had been stunned. Of course, stunning prior to bleeding, which has always been practised in the case of large bovines for reasons of safety, is now compulsory for all animals on humanitarian grounds; *a fortiori*, any ill-treatment before slaughtering is prohibited and penalised. Infringements of the regulations may [in France] be recorded and punished by representatives of the SPA [*Société protectrice des animaux*] or the OABA (a specialised charity [*Oeuvre d'assistance aux bêtes des abattoirs*] founded in 1961).

Safety standards for personnel and animals, laying down safety regulations for lairage, tools, and equipment. For instance, unloading platforms for animals must have an optimal fall; their surfaces, like the floors of cattle pens and slaughterhalls, must not be allowed to become slippery or inundated; slaughterers must wear metal gloves to protect them from injury, and so on.

Finally, economic standards regarding the taxes and fees levied per head slaughtered but also with regard to limits governing the trimming of carcasses (to remove fat) before weighing or the obligation to leave the tail attached to carcasses of large bovines (to prevent fraud).

This very cursory survey gives sufficient indication that nothing here is left to chance, not only because, as with all foodstuffs, a great many requirements come together, but also because 'meat – like bread – has been and still is subject to a level of supervision that makes it a political commodity' (Chaudieu 1980, p. 42) – assuming, of course, that it is not inevitably 'political', for what animal sacrifice does not involved the entire *polis*, either directly or indirectly? To put it another way, because it comes to us by way of the killing of animals, meat is necessarily 'political'. The fact is that the slaughter of domestic mammals has never been left to the individual imagination.

This elaborate grid of regulations explains why as an ethnologist studying abattoirs I first had to get across to people not so much who I was and what I was after as what I was not. Where it is customary to use the word *enquête* ['investigation', but also 'inquiry'] in connection with a piece of ethnological fieldwork (e.g., the 'tools of investigation' [*outils d'enquête*] discussed in Cresswell and Godelier 1976), with a view to distinguishing between the collection [*quête*] of information and the analysis thereof, in the abattoir context it is better to talk of an *étude* ['study']. An *enquête*, here, will be looking into compliance with standards and may result in offenders being punished. In other words, it was not possible to establish any kind of trust (or at least remove the initial mistrust accorded as a matter of principle) until I had made it crystal-clear that I had not been sent, either directly or indirectly, by any supervisory authority. In this respect the patronage of the Ministry of Culture, the terms of the brief, namely 'popular naturalist knowledge', and the purely academic nature and avowed 'uselessness' of my project were far better credentials than any anxious attempt at self-justification on alleged utilitarian grounds would have been. So one's normal professional code of ethics needed to be observed very strictly here, and interviewees often wanted to be able to verify that such would indeed be the case. I was free, presumably, to publish anything I

5 General view of La Villette abattoirs in 1890

understood (or thought I understood) in the realm of theory but not everything I knew in the realm of fact (which might constitute an infringement of one or another regulation).

Exile and euphemisms

The dissociation between butchery and slaughtering, which today is complete, could only be accomplished by banishing the abattoir to a site outside the city walls. ('*Aux portes de Paris*' are the first words to appear on the screen and to be taken up by the commentary of Franju's *Le sang des bêtes*). However, that exile could equally be construed as a confinement, as one authority has pointed out, showing that 'the important thing is the notion of example: concealing the killing in order not to give people ideas', (Agulhon 1981, p. 85). Indeed, while it certainly had to do with a town-planning policy concerned about public hygiene, exiling the abattoir was also, through that very policy, an expression of the profound shift in sensibilities with regard to such realities as death (human or animal), suffering, violence, waste and disease, 'miasmas', and finally animals themselves, which were increasingly coming to be seen as 'lesser brethren' (Agulhon 1981; Ariès 1977; Corbin 1978, 1982, 1984; Pélosse 1981–2; Thomas 1983; Vigarello 1985). It so happens that animal slaughter offers a perfect synthesis of all this, almost a textbook example, in fact.

The shift in sensibilities found notable expression in the 1833 ban on animal fights in Paris (and subsequently in the prolonged – and still current – controversy concerning bullfights) and in the creation in France in 1846 of the animal-protection society SPA (in Great Britain, the RSPCA had been in existence since 1824); it received official recognition in 1850 with the passing of the Grammont Law penalising ill-treatment of domestic animals.

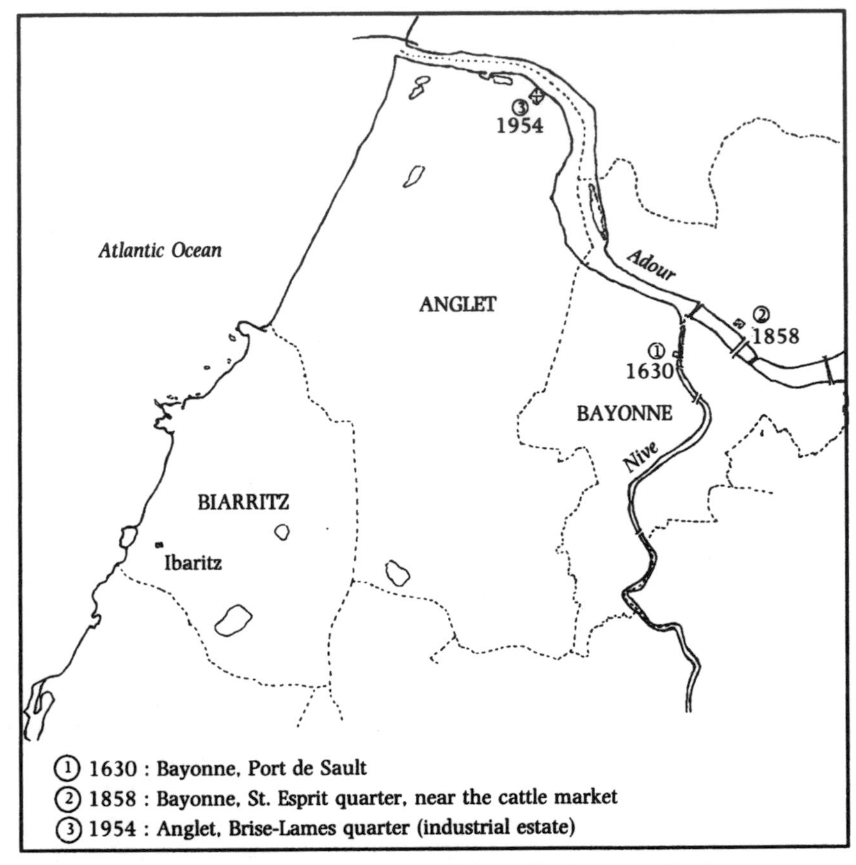

6 Successive sitings of abattoirs in the Biarritz-Anglet-Bayonne district

From then on all transporting and killing of animals in towns became unacceptable, and these activities had to be banished beyond the gates. This centrifugal movement, already begun between 1808 and 1818, became steadily more pronounced. In Paris, the La Villette (built 1865–9) and Vaugirard (1897) abattoirs replaced those built at the beginning of the century, which had meanwhile been reached and swallowed up by urban sprawl. In the provinces, the same exile occurred slightly later, but what we find invariably is that abattoirs were moved, sometimes on two occasions, farther and farther from urban centres. The case of Bayonne and Biarritz was entirely typical of what happened to abattoirs almost everywhere (see figures 6–8).

Henceforth slaughtering was invisible – the more so, in fact, as technical improvements made it possible to conjure away more and more of the age-old signs of the business. The traveller must pass very close to an abattoir before a faintly acrid smell perhaps catches his attention; the surrounding

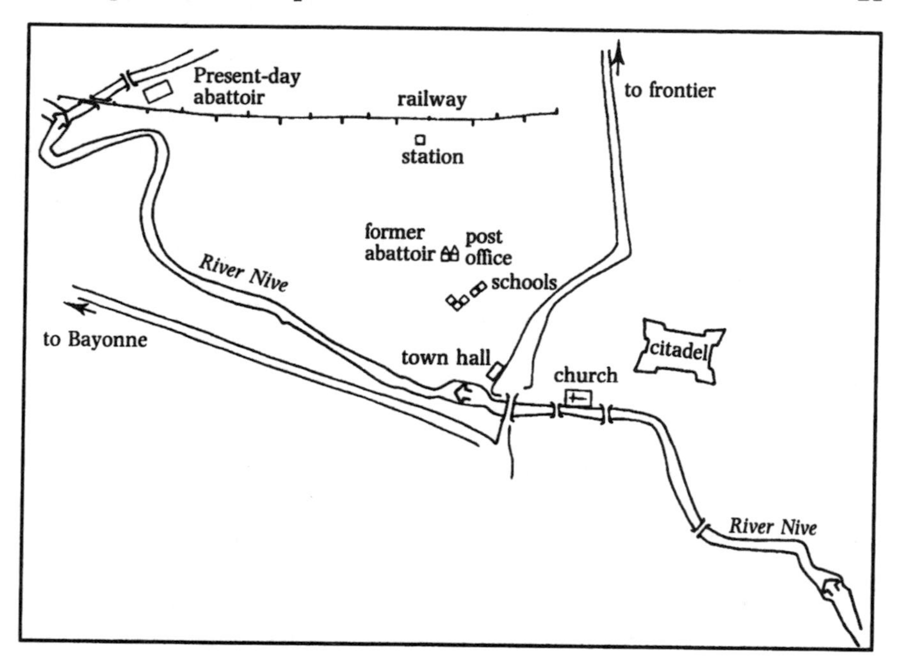

7 Successive sitings of the St-Jean-Pied-de-Port abattoir

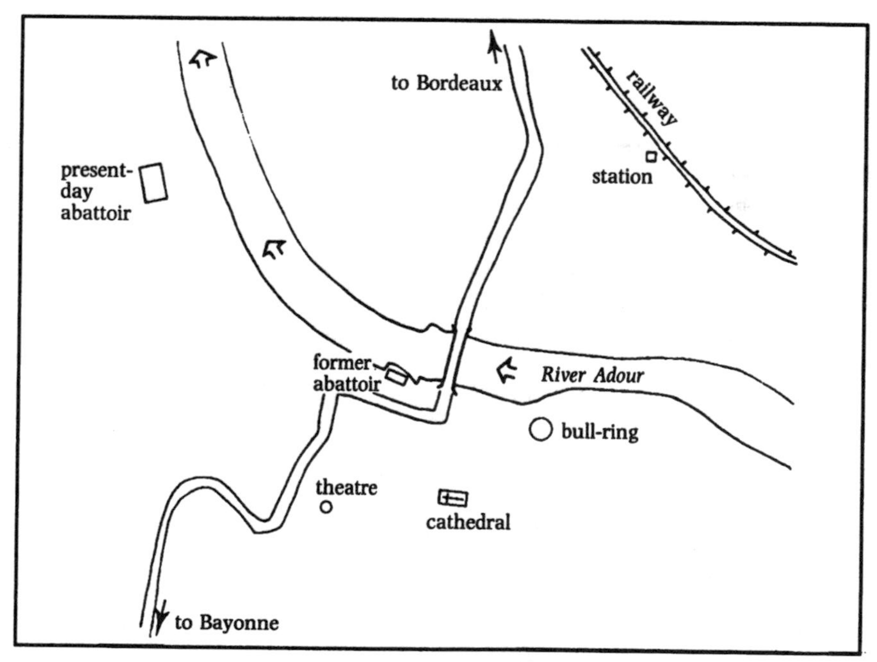

8 Successive sitings of the Aire-sur-l'Adour abattoir

walls allow little evidence to escape of the almost clandestine slaughter of animals happening inside. Abattoirs built in the early nineteenth century occasionally (and ingenously?) inscribed their façades with the legend '*Liberté-Égalité-Fraternité*' (Gascar 1973, p. 104), but nowadays all you see is a high wall with a number of rooftops peeping above it; it is rare for the entrance to bear any kind of inscription, and even rarer for there to be signposts showing how to get there. Those who use the place know, and the general public neither needs nor wishes to know. The livestock trucks and refrigerator vans seen driving in or out or parked beside the carcass loading platforms near the entrance gate suggest that this establishment has something to do with animals and meat, but the essential operation is quite invisible from outside and there is nothing to invite one in; in fact there will be a sign saying '*Interdit au publique*' ('No admittance').

The exiling of the abattoir, by confining slaughtering to an enclosed space, simultaneously satisfied the need to monitor, control, and if necessary punish (to take up once again the themes developed by Michel Foucault): to monitor operations, in order progressively to eliminate acts of violence, and to monitor the quality and marketing of the meat, in order to prevent fraud. Simultaneously, treatises on meat inspection began to be published (e.g., Baillet 1880; it was the start of a whole literature that merits its own extended analysis).

The final corollary of this exile/confinement is the concentration of slaughtering activity and the reduction of the number of abattoirs. The quantities dealt with were henceforth on an industrial scale and called for suitable organisation. It was a development that led, for example, to the remarkable 'vertical' abattoirs of Chicago. However, we shall see how this process of industrialisation, inevitable if we wish to be spared the daily spectacle of animals being slaughtered, may itself engender fresh fantasies (to which recent history has no doubt helped to lend a certain consistency).

To sum up: from this point on, slaughtering was required to be industrial, that is to say large scale and anonymous; it must be non-violent (ideally: painless); and it must be invisible (ideally: non-existent). It must be as if it were not.

However, the 'no-place' where this massive and methodically repudiated slaughter nevertheless went on had a name, which still gave it too much existence. This term, which in its metaphorical senses had become at least as violent as *boucherie*, to which it added an industrial connotation, certainly responded initially to an attempt at euphemisation. After all, there was nothing to prevent the old term *tuerie* from being retained to designate the new slaughterhouses, keeping *boucherie* for retail meat outlets (as indeed happened). However, the term *abattoir* was coined, together with a new acceptation for *abattage* (or *abatage*).

The general meaning of *abattre* is 'to cause to fall' or 'to bring down that which is standing'. It is primarily a term in forestry, where it refers to felling; subsequently, it came to be used in the mineral world, where it denoted the action of detaching material from the walls of a mine tunnel. It also belongs to the vocabulary of veterinary surgery, and particularly when applied to a horse it means to lay the animal down in order to operate on it or more generally to give it medical attention. In 1878 the *Littré* dictionary also gave this definition:

In terms of military administration, *abatage* of animals is the killing of animals destined to feed the troops ... In terms of sanitary policy, *abatage* is the killing of large domestic animals, either because they are old or incurably ill, or as a precaution when they are suspected of having or have actually contracted a contagious disease.

The 1961 edition of the dictionary likewise does not mention the precise meaning (the killing of animals to provide food for men, not just the troops) that would be the logical extension of the definition given elsewhere, in all editions, under the headword *abattoir* (see above, p. 15).

The *abattage* performed in *abattoirs* should therefore be understood as an analogy and an example of litotes. With reference to the vocabulary of forestry, it suggests an analogy between the slaughter of animals and the felling of trees, both of which involve bringing into a recumbent position something that was standing erect; the former *tuerie* becomes like woodcutting, the animal is vegetalised, as it were, the slaughterer becomes a woodcutter, and blood is almost edulcorated into sap. With reference to the vocabulary of veterinary medicine, euphemisation occurs by way of litotes, the analogy of the recumbent posture achieved making it possible to gloss over the crucial difference between treatment and slaughter. It is perhaps not by chance that this process of euphemisation first appeared in a service in which horses played a major role.

Using the derivative *abattoir* meant that the terms *tuerie* and *écorcherie* (both in use for 'slaughterhouse') could be avoided. However, it is in the nature of certain euphemisms to fail: 'If the idea is one of those of which the social and moral norm disapproves, the euphemism will not last; itself contaminated, it will need to be renewed' (Benveniste [1949] 1966, p. 309). In the same article Emile Benveniste recalls 'the euphemistic origin' of the French verb *tuer*, derived from the Latin *tutare*, as in the expression *ignem tutare*, 'to calm or quell (fire)'. *Abattre* did not contrive to euphemise *tuer*, the latter having eventually become too brutal, but *abattoir* singularly failed to euphemise *tuerie* in any lasting way, and no fresh term has yet replaced it. All that is left is the disapproval and the metaphorical usages through which the worn-out euphemism admits its failure.

We find confirmation of this process of wear in the descriptions accompanying the *abattoir* article in successive editions of Larousse encyclopaedias (see figures 9–12), which show how the term has gradually had to be

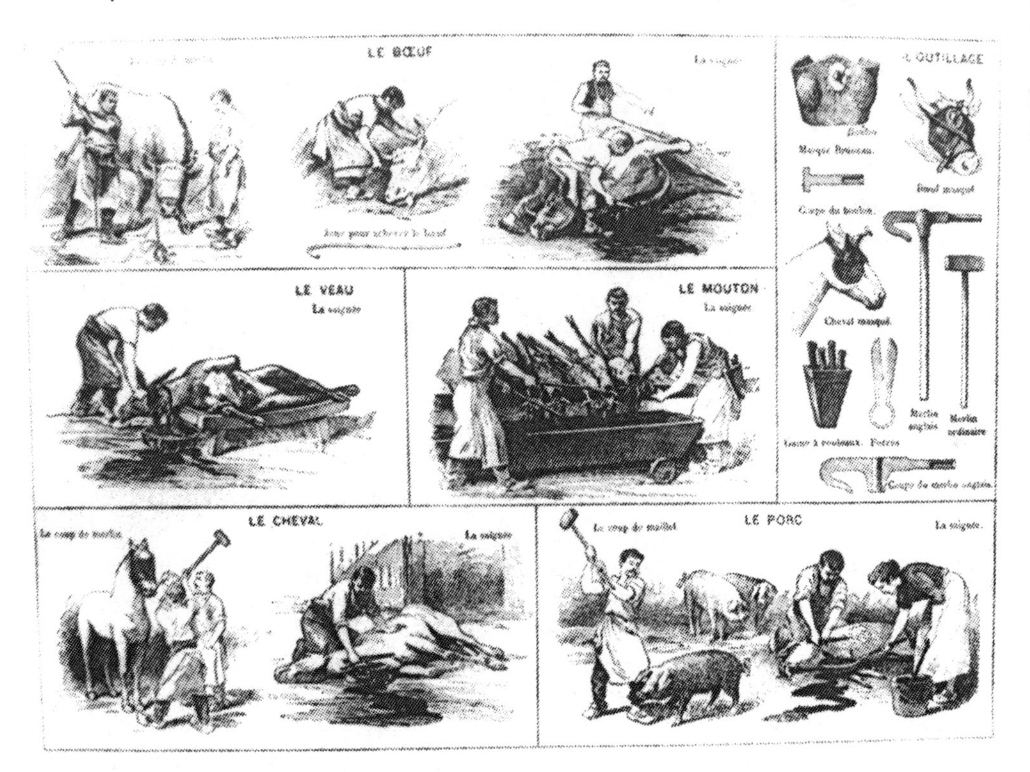

9 Plate from *Nouveau Larousse illustré*, undated (probably 1905) vol. 1, p. 7, article *Abatage*

Slaughter of animals for butchering, from photographs taken at the abattoirs of La Villette and Villejuif (Paris).

emptied of all precise concrete representation in order to keep it 'presentable'.

Take the 1905, 1928, 1960, and 1982 editions. The first two, true to their encyclopaedic aspirations, leave nothing to the imagination as regards informing readers about the methods employed; the equipment is shown in detail, and stunning and slaughtering are quite uncensored. The 1928 edition even adds three illustrations depicting the abattoirs of Chicago. The ideology of progress means that everything can be shown. In 1960, the *abattage* and *abattoir* articles are illustrated separately. The three principal meanings of *abattage* ('forestry', 'butchery', 'mining') are illustrated side by side. Photographs have replaced drawings, there are no close-ups of the equipment used, and the only illustration of the slaughtering process avoids depicting the act: what we see, accompanied by the caption 'bleeding a bullock in the vertical position', is the blood being drained. The way in which the *abattoir* article is illustrated is even more revealing. Here the ideology of progress is content to compare a plate from Diderot's eighteenth-century

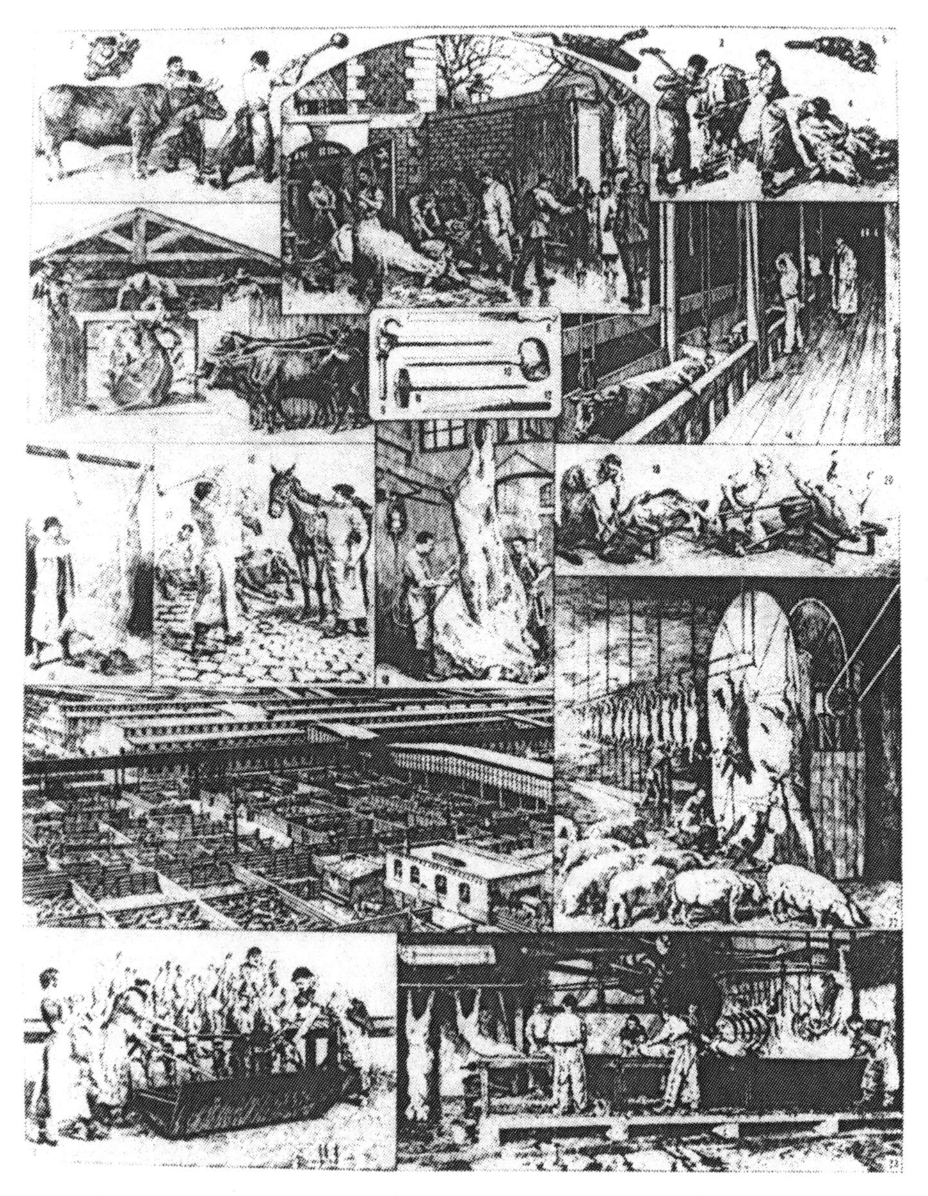

10 Plate from *Larousse du xxe siècle*, 1928, vol. 1, p. 7, article *Abattoir*

Abattoir: (1) Slaughtering a bullock using mallet and Bruneau mask; (2) The Bruneau mask in place; (3) Slaughterman using a poleaxe (*merlin anglais*); (4) Inserting the pithing rod; (5) Compressed-air pistol (humane killer); (6) Knife-holster (shop); (7) Jewish scalding room, showing invalids arriving to drink fresh blood: (8) Jewish sacrificial knife; (9) Poleaxe; (10) Mallet; (11) Sledge; (12) Bleeder's knife; (13) Slaughter in a Paraguayan *saladero*; (14) Bullocks being slaughtered in Chicago; (15) Veterinary inspection; (16), (17) Horse being slaughtered and bled; (18) Power flaying; (19), (20) Calf being bled and inflated; (21) Livestock pens in Chicago; (22) Pigs being slaughtered and bled in Chicago; (23) Scalding tub and dehairing table for pigs; (24) Sheep being bled.

11 Plates from *Grand Larousse encyclopédique*, 1960
(upper plate – vol. 1, p. 7, article *Abattage*; lower plate – vol. 1, p. 8, article *Abattoir*)

Encyclopédie (the 'butchery' article) with an architect's drawing of a contemporary slaughterhall, shown empty and therefore clean and peaceful. The commentary underlines the contrast between the old method of slaughtering, with the butcher confronting the animal, and 'one of the halls' of the Marseille abattoirs in which '200 calves, 400 bovines, 1,000 pigs, and 1,800 sheep can be slaughtered in a day' [using the French 'passive' construction '*l'on peut tuer* ...']. The quantities cited depersonalise the activity and hence appear to absolve it, and we are scarcely aware of what is actually happening here, invited as we are to admire the technical skill and rest our eyes on the ideal cleanliness of these 'halls'.

However, it was still possible to go one better. The 1982 edition contrives to explain everything while at the same time showing nothing and saying nothing. The illustration is a mere diagram of the 'principle of operation', and the text of the article is the purest understatement presented with the soberest good taste, the technicality of the language employed not only paying tribute to the ideology of progress but actually managing to obscure the thing to which it is being applied. The only really explicit (and disturbing) words are used to define the metaphorical meaning by referring back to 'familiar' vocabulary:

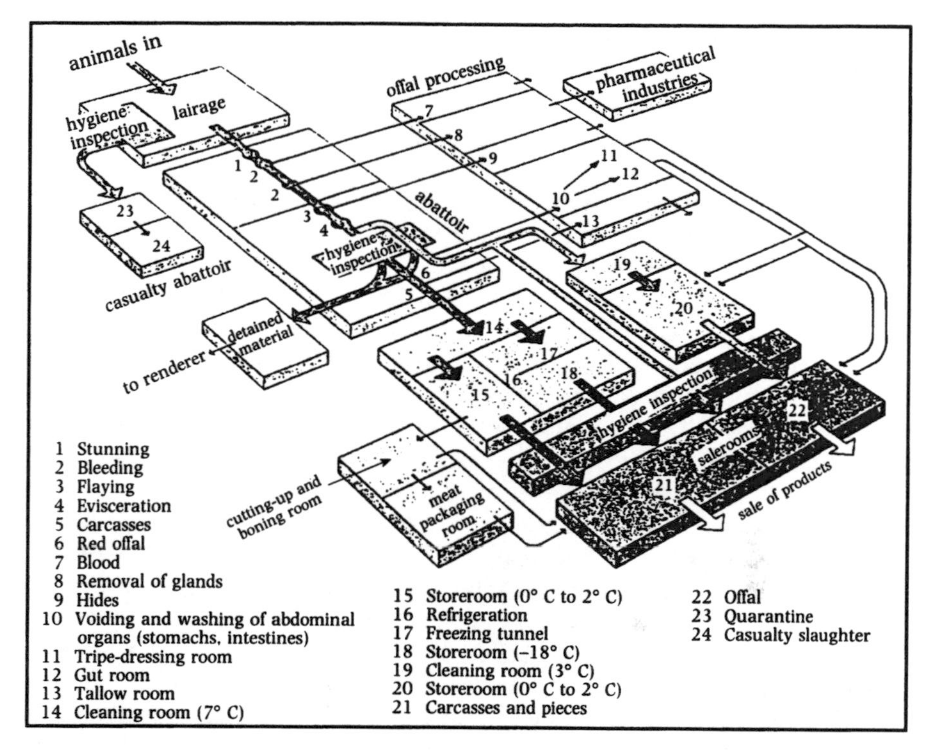

12 Abattoir: layout and operation of an abattoir for bovines
(Diagram from *Grand Dictionnaire encyclopédique Larousse*, 1982, vol. 1, p. 8, article *Abattoir*)

'place where men are massacred, particularly in wartime: "*envoyer des soldats à l'abattoir*" ["to send soldiers to be slaughtered"]'. As if the familiarity (not to say excessiveness) of the metaphor undermined the reality of the horror it evokes, with the dubious dysphemic image becoming a fresh euphemism!

So the separation of butchery and slaughter, of meat and the killing of animals, is based jointly on the banishment of abattoirs and an attempt at euphemisation. This initial disjunction was to lead to others, inside abattoirs themselves but also outside them.

Expelled from town and city centres, abattoirs sprang up in the suburbs, in outlying industrial estates, classified as (in the words of a decree of 15 April 1838) 'inconvenient, insalubrious, and dangerous' establishments like many other industries and accordingly required, as regards their siting, to seek planning permission and submit to the process of public inquiry. Forced out of towns, they were equally banished from the countryside. Condemned to an existence on the fringes of urban and rural society, they were cut off from the consumer and the stockbreeder alike. The former could henceforth be unaware of the origin of the meat he was eating, the latter of the destination of the animal he reared.

However, the breeder may himself be a consumer, which introduces a significant difference between them.

Anonymous flesh

The urban consumer is never, in terms of his daily alimentary experience, brought face to face with the animal. His steps take him no farther than the butcher's shop where he buys his meat. For him, the origin of that meat is entirely hidden from view; so far as he is concerned, the banishment of the abattoir has fully achieved the effect intended. The town-dweller tucks serenely into his meat, fortifying himself with the 'sanguine' aspect that according to Roland Barthes constitutes the *raison d'être* of beefsteak (Barthes [1957] 1970, p. 78), because he is spared the sight of animals being slaughtered. He consumes a *substance* [French achieves the transformation through the use of the particle *de*, as in *il mange* du *veau*, du *boeuf*...; English of course uses different words for animal and meat, e.g. calf/veal] that is anonymous, anodine, and available in adequate quantities – provided, at least, that his economic circumstances are not such as to restrict his enjoyment of it. Hygiene controls ensure the meat is harmless, and at a more subjective level the consumer likes to 'trust' his butcher. But has he, in fact, any alternative?

Probably a predilection for meat-eating is automatically accompanied by a vague sense of its peculiarity, although the feeling rarely achieves the clarity that, for example, Italo Calvino gives it in his novel *Palomar*:

> A respectful devotion towards everything connected with the flesh guides Mr Palomar as he prepares to purchase three steaks. He pauses between the marble counters of the butcher's shop as in a temple, aware of the fact that his individual existence and the culture to which he belongs are conditioned by this place ...
>
> While acknowledging in the carcass of beef that hangs there the person of his own quartered brother and in the cutting of the loin a wound that mutilates his own flesh, he knows that he is a carnivore, conditioned by his alimentary tradition to grasp, when in a butcher's, the promise of gustatory bliss and to imagine, looking at the blood-red slices, the stripes that the flames will leave on the steaks as they grill and the pleasure that his teeth will feel as they sever the smooth fibre.
>
> One feeling does not exclude another, and Palomar's state of mind as he queues at the butcher's is one of simultaneous controlled delight and fear, desire and respect, preoccupation with self and universal compassion: it is the state of mind that for others, perhaps, finds expression in prayer (Calvino 1983).

No doubt many of us will recognise ourselves in Palomar as in a caricature that gets rather too close to the truth, bringing right out into the open what normally remains buried – if not in the unconscious, at least in unawareness.

It is different for the stockbreeder and, by extension, for all whose trade puts them in the position of not losing sight of the animal in meat.

The fate of animals raised 'for slaughter' is sealed from the moment of their birth. They are fed and sold to be killed as soon as they reach the desired stage of growth. It is unusual for a stockbreeder to wish (or to have the opportunity) to accompany his animals to the abattoir. When he does so, it is in order to 'check on the yield', in particular to ascertain how much profit he has made on each animal by comparing carcass weight with live weight. In other words, it is for purely zootechnical purposes, and experienced breeders and/or those who have kept faith with traditional methods will not even need to check. If a breeder 'has the eye' he will 'not be in for any surprises'. The expert knows; he does not need to see the figures. In any event, the animal bred for slaughter usually disappears from view as soon as it is sold.

On the other hand, animals destined for domestic consumption return to the stockbreeder after slaughter in the form of carcasses. Pigs may still be slaughtered at home for purely family consumption, but more and more farmers now have their animals slaughtered at the abattoir: 'It's easier as well as quicker; it causes less upset.' In such cases it is not in fact unusual for the owner of the animal to follow the whole operation closely with something approaching the blend of 'desire and respect' described by Calvino. It is a question of 'seeing how they go about it' in order to effect the transformation within the rules of the art. But it is also a question of watching to see that one's own animal is not swapped for another. This is about more than simply the proprietory instinct; what is finding expression here is the desire, clearly enunciated, to 'know what one is eating', and a person can only really know this if he is able to refer what he is eating to a very precisely identifiable animal that he has raised for the purpose, knowing what it has eaten itself. This does not imply any pleasure in seeing it slaughtered ('if you want to eat it you've got to kill it'), but the need to 'know what one is eating' takes precedence, and acceptance of the killing of animals for food is immemorial among farmers (except as regards an animal not normally, i.e., from birth, destined for slaughter, in which case the attitude is quite different). Indeed, then the very terms in which the animal's end is expressed are different: it is sold not 'for butchering' but 'to be killed' ['*pour la mort*'], or sometimes it will have 'gone to be killed' ['*il est parti pour la mort*'].

The same identification of meat by reference to the actual animal is found among meat wholesalers or retailers who buy cattle for slaughter. Not that they are able to make the identification with the same precision as a stockbreeder, who will have raised the animal himself, but it is to the properties of the live animal that the properties of the meat are attributed, and the traditional 'feeling of the points' ('*maniements*'; Déterville 1982, p. 17; see figure 13), still practised by fatstock buyers, aims to anticipate on the live animal what its meat will be like. Here are just a few sentences from the long and picturesque description that Chaudieu gives of it in a book entitled 'From haunch of bear to hamburger, or the curious story of meat':

13 Feeling the points at Smithfield Agricultural Show, from *The Graphic*, 1895 (reproduced in Chaudieu 1970)

The ceremony of the feeling of the points began. With it the classic movements, codified by time, by means of which the density of the muscle and the delicacy of the fat layer and the 'grain of the meat' may be appreciated 'under the skin', took on the look of caresses ... Then, planting himself firmly at some distance from the animal, he assessed its nature, the instincts that would also make the meat delicate or coarse, sapid or insipid. His judgement was completed ... He had divined the 'soul' of this meat while it was still alive (Chaudieu 1980, p. 101).

It is a similar desire to find the properties of the animal in the meat that seems to account for the liking that certain *aficionados* of the corrida exhibit for the meat of bulls that have fought in the ring. Indeed, as food it apparently has no great gastronomic qualities, as those same *aficionados* will admit, but clearly eating *toro* is quite different from eating beef – to the point where, unable to attend the corrida themselves (seats, particularly in the shade, are expensive), people will make do with casseroling one of these raging heroes of the southern Sunday afternoon and be able to say, 'At least we'll have eaten a bit of it.'

There are two opposing logics here: that of the eater of a substance, and that of the eater of animals. Closer inspection, however, shows that they are in fact interdependent.

The thing that separates them is the difference between slaughter on a massive, industrial scale, which for that reason is harrowing and is therefore kept out of sight, and an individual act of killing that preserves a link, however tenuous and even purely imaginary, between eater and eaten. We shall see that this difference has consequences inside the abattoir itself. For the moment, let us simply note that, while no one takes pleasure in the act of killing for its own sake, at least one-to-one slaughter, in which the roles of animal and man persist right up until the act of killing, is easier to accept than industrial slaughter. Indeed, the latter has the effect of eliminating landmarks, imposing an anonymity on the animals (as well as on the men who face them) and giving rise to a general lack of differentiation that is experienced as disorienting: anything, including the worst, seems possible. Moreover, it ceases to be possible to attribute to individual pathologies or to pure fantasy the analogies expressed on a number of occasions, inside abattoirs themselves, between the mass slaughter of animals and equally large-scale exterminations of human beings.

It is this frightening lack of differentiation that the town-dweller wishes to know nothing of (for the very reason that he senses it) and that others for various reasons seek to avoid. This is the thing that in the two opposing logics lies at the heart of the problem.

We see now why the disjunctions are necessary: urbanisation and the consumption of large quantities of meat lead directly to the creation of abattoirs as places set apart, where the inevitable occurs. All these disjunctions invite and combine with one another to keep the mass killing of animals at a reasonable distance. They never entirely succeed in doing so because the necessity is as imperious (at least until a person decides to become vegetarian) as the values that disown it. Hence the ceaseless multiplication of efforts (i.e., separations) with the aim of circumscribing the thing rejected and narrowing the field of ambiguity, the place, and the fatal moment in which order (identified with 'the clean'), in the process of becoming established, is

I 'IT WAS LIKE STRING'

'There are people who'd sell their bodies to eat a bit of bull from the ring! Pure snobbery, that is. I was in Aigues-Mortes one day when there'd been a bullfight. Well, the fuss in all the restaurants! It just wasn't true! Like when you used to get prize beef! When there was prize beef they'd sell a hundred times as much of it, a hundred times as many pieces as made up one animal. All right, I remember this time I was in Aigues-Mortes, my wife was with me . . . well, there'd been a bullfight. In the restaurant, there it was on the menu – beef casserole from the animal that had been killed the day before . . . they even gave its name, the bull's name, like a V.I.P. We wanted to try what it was like. All right, the gravy was fine, but the meat was like string. No, it's no better. It's lean, of course it is, it's a fighting bull [taureau] *. . . It's just local snobbery. Oh no, not one of your top-quality meats, fighting bull.'*

still somewhat precarious. It is very much as if the initial separation between killing and meat had triggered a process of repeated fissions forming a kind of spiral of avoidance of a reality and a meaning that are too raw, the centre of the spiral and the force behind it being the very thing that it is trying to avoid – forever unsuccessfully, and for good reason.

We shall find this process of repeated fissions at work inside abattoirs too, even at the point where one would expect to see it come up against (and possibly be frustrated by) the nub of the problem, namely the precise moment at which death is administered.

2

FLAYING THE ANIMAL: THE DISJUNCTIONS INVOLVED

What the regulations say

Every animal taken to the abattoir must be slaughtered there. It is strictly forbidden for it to come out alive. Once it has passed through the entrance gate, its fate is irreversibly sealed and its path can only be one way.

Every animal must be killed by bleeding, and this must be done in an abattoir; these two conditions must be fulfilled for the meat to be deemed suitable for human consumption. So it is forbidden to slaughter otherwise than by bleeding, which must be 'complete and rapid'. An animal that has been bled may be flayed or skinned away from the abattoir, but with very few exceptions, which are strictly defined and under the control of a vet, there will be a ban on its carcass being prepared for human consumption. The carcass will be confiscated and, depending on the decision of the abattoir inspector, either set aside for animal food or destroyed with the solid waste in the renderers' melters.

Every animal must be stunned before being bled, except for certain precisely regulated dispensations, particularly in connection with ritual slaughter.[1] Stunning is done with a captive-bolt pistol, which perforates the cranium, or in the case of pigs and sheep with electrodes, through which an electric shock is administered. Use of the poleaxe [which French calls the *merlin anglais*] has been banned since 1964. While the technical documents speak of *insensibilisation* or *anesthésie* [both meaning 'anaesthesia'], they do occasionally also use the term *assommage* [stunning]; this is in fact the term most commonly used, along with *électrocution*.

Every animal must be immobilised and stunned on the floor, then suspended before being killed by bleeding. On the other hand, while the job of flaying is usually done with the carcass suspended, this is not compulsory

[1] In the four *départements* covered by the study, none of the abattoirs practises slaughter according to the Jewish rite. This is because they lack the equipment required to respect the demands of the ritual as well as those concerning the humane treatment of animals. An abattoir will be fitted out with such equipment only if a fairly large tonnage needs to be slaughtered in this way. Consequently, ritual slaughter is concentrated at a small number of abattoirs. Slaughter in accordance with the Muslim rite poses similar problems.

and some abattoirs are still equipped with flaying cradles (see figure 61), particularly for calves and sheep. The requirement that animals be bled in suspension has to do with technical considerations in that the hanging position ensures bleeding will be successful; it rules out the sort of incomplete bleeding [known as '*coffrage*' in French; literally 'coffering'] that beginners do not always manage to avoid.

Any animal found to be sick or deemed hygienically suspect will be kept apart from the others, in quarantine, and must be slaughtered on separate premises; the carcass will be kept in a separate refrigerated room set aside for meat that has been detained or seized by customs.

All meat declared unfit for human consumption must be detained and denatured. Denaturing will be achieved by various processes, depending on whether the meat concerned is to be sent to the renderer to be destroyed (that is to say, sterilised and turned into livestock feed or fertiliser) or recovered for animal food, either as raw meat or as manufactured pet food. As with the detention of confiscated meat, the object of denaturing is to avoid any misappropriation. It consists essentially in making the meat unfit for use as food, even for animals, by first slashing it, for instance, and then pouring disinfectant or paraffin over it; or it may consist in simply making the meat look repellent by injecting it with a solution of lucerne flour in water, where the meat is destined for animal consumption.

It is important to bear all these 'musts' in mind if we are to understand certain arrangements made in connection with the slaughter of animals. Clearly, indeed, they all have rational justifications on grounds of public hygiene, worker safety, the quality and conservation of the meat produced, or the protection of the animals. The principal goal pursued, however, is that of the quality (in health terms, at least) of the main end-product, namely meat for human consumption. It follows that care must be taken to ensure that the meat remains wholesome and clean, which means methodically separating it from every source of contamination and tainting.

Yet rational though these requirements may be, they are not without a symbolic dimension as well. Generally speaking, 'clean' is never a straightforward, objective reality, even less an objective datum. Permanently caught up in an ordering of the world, it involves more than strictly rational representations. This is so even (and perhaps especially) when it can claim to be based on such representations.

> When we have detached pathogenesis and hygiene from our ideas about dirt, all we are left with is our old definition: it is something that is not in the right place ... Dirt is thus never a single, isolated phenomenon. Where there is dirt, there is system (Douglas 1967).

Any slaughtering operation consists in isolating the edible flesh, the meat, from the animal on the hoof. However, this is achieved in different ways, depending on the actual resources available to each abattoir, which may vary widely. Even if every degree of technological modernisation is observed, we can nevertheless distinguish between new or renovated abattoirs and others that are older, less well equipped, and still lumbered with working methods that under restructuring are condemned to disappear. We need to look at how one and the same end can be achieved by different means as well as at what sort of logic governs those different means.

'Clean' and 'dirty'

A modern abattoir has two entrances; they may both be in the façade of the building, or one may be round the back. Whichever is the case, they give on to two quite distinct zones. The interior of an abattoir is not a homogeneous space; it is a directional space. There is a 'front' and a 'rear' or, to put it in the terms used in official, printed discourse, there is a 'clean sector' and a 'dirty sector'.

The 'front' is the presentable aspect, with refrigerator vans lining the loading platforms where the pink carcasses, neatly stamped, firm, and fresh-looking, whole, in halves, or in quarters, dangling from an overhead track or hoisted on the shoulders of white-clad, hooded porters, are sorted for delivery to the retail butchers or shipped to far-off destinations.

The 'rear' is the hidden side, where the cattle trucks arrive full of animals that, after a journey of greater or lesser length, are unloaded at the gates of pens or taken straight to the waiting areas that give access to the slaughter-hall. It is also the sector where the empty cattle trucks are disinfected, where the dunghill stands beside the dirty water filtration plant, and where various sheds house the hides being salted or the waste containers that are awaiting collection by the renderer.

Clearly, the 'dirty sector' is the realm of the warm, the moist, the living, of smells and secretions, of the biological threat that needs constantly to be contained and cleaned up. The 'clean sector', on the other hand, is where everything is inert, bloodless, trimmed, and stabilised by cold.

Between the two sectors (and as it were above them) are the offices of the management, responsible, ideally, for seeing and knowing all and for guaranteeing order and the overall success of the operation.

Also between the two sectors (but at the most sensitive point of the whole arrangement) is the slaughterhall. Those who work therein give it the same orientation as the sectors outside in terms of 'front' and 'rear'. At the 'rear', the animals enter the stunning pen, where they are slaughtered; at the 'front' the carcasses arrive to be weighed before being moved on to the cooling rooms and finally the storerooms. 'Front' and 'rear' are crucially determined by the path taken by the animals, which is one way; that path leaves 'behind' it the space it has travelled through, at the same time as the men whose work makes them move forward also leave 'behind' them what has been done.

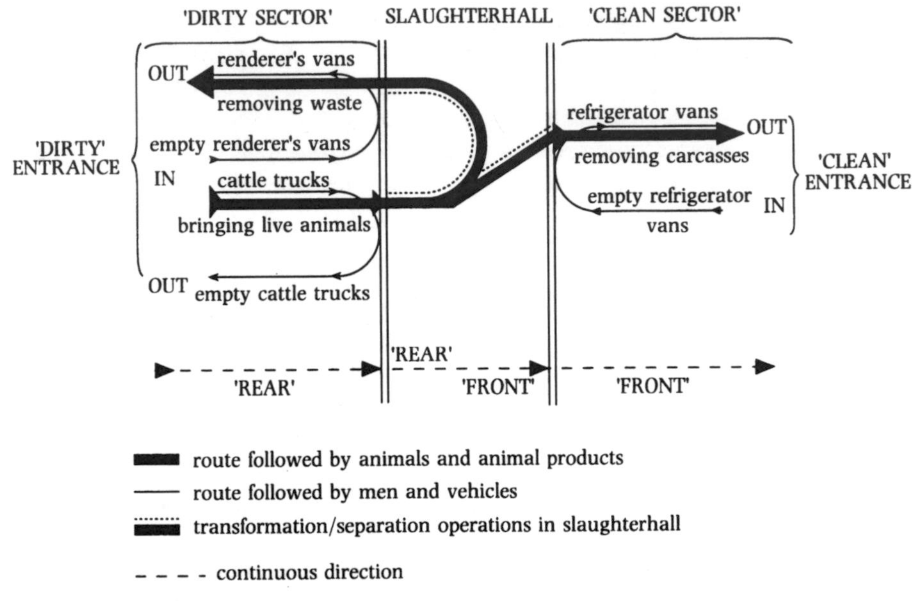

14 Diagram showing routes in a slaughterhall

Time and space are here reconstituted in the form of a chiasmus: before in time = 'behind' in space, while after in time = 'in front of' in space. The order in which the operations are performed unfolds in a space that the animals pass through, and the rear/front (behind/in front of) antithesis draws its meaning and consistency from the irreversibility (so far as the animals are concerned) of the passage through the slaughterhall.

For anyone outside the slaughterhall, however, the central position of the latter clearly isolates it between the sectors, leaving it belonging to neither. This is clear on plans of abattoirs, whether actual or ideal (see figures 14–17). It is also visible in very concrete terms in the double rotation described around the hall by the lorries circulating in each sector, which go out the same way as they came in, keeping the hall supplied with animals or collecting the products it turns out (manufactures, as represented by the carcasses, and scrap, as represented by the waste). The slaughterhall, which is always avoided, is the principle of their movement and the principle of the division into sectors; in other words, it performs a disjunctive function. This can be represented in diagrammatic form (figure 14).

We see from the diagram that, as the (materially isolated) scene of a transformation, the slaughterhall is at the source of both a uniform orientation of space (front/rear, in front of/behind) and a separation of that space into distinct sectors. As the site of a work process, it governs a continuous spatial

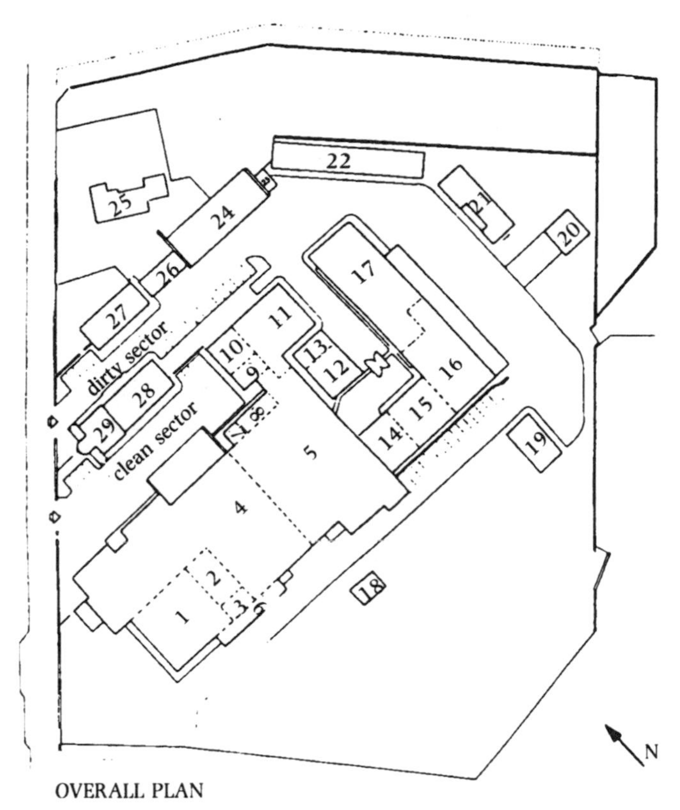

15 Layout of an abattoir processing more then 11,000 tonnes a year.
'Clean' and 'dirty' sectors are clearly distinguished

progression; however, since that work process consists in a radical separation, it introduces a discontinuity by, as it were, contaminating the space in which it is performed.

As a scene of transformation, the slaughterhall is also an eminently ambiguous place (a 'fringe' place [*lieu de marge*], in Van Gennep's terminology) where the slaughtered beast is no longer quite an animal and not yet meat. It 'floats between two worlds' (Van Gennep [1909] 1981, pp. 23–4). We can apply to it wholesale the analyses that Van Gennep gives of 'certain fringe cases that possess a certain autonomy', cases in which, 'for a period of time that may vary in length, the subject of the ceremony should not touch the ground' (*ibid.*, p. 285). Indeed, suspension prior to bleeding is obligatory, and henceforth the body will never touch the floor again, whether flaying is done from an overhead track or on cradles. In very general terms, we find that even the most ancient (and apparently least hygienic) practices

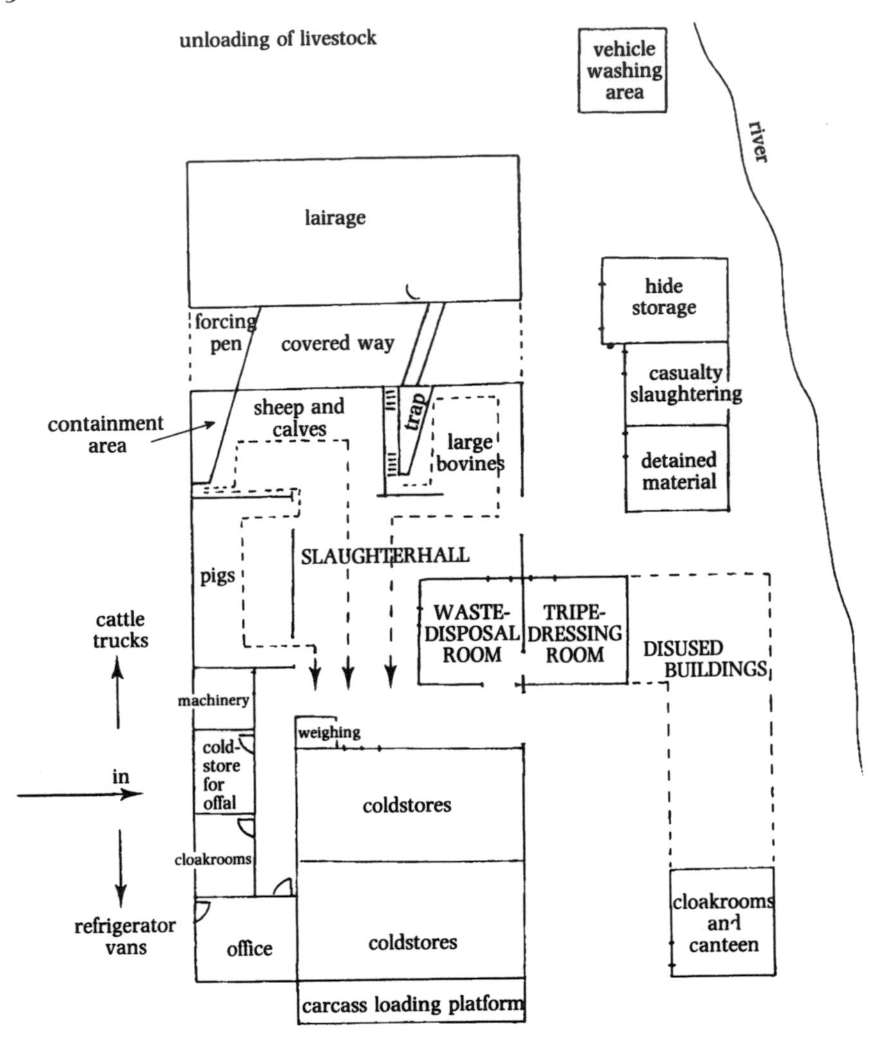

16 Layout of an abattoir recently renovated to process approximately 2,500 tonnes a year.

Only one entrance, but afterwards cattle trucks go one way (dirty sector) and refrigerator vans the other (clean sector)

throughout the world take care to keep meat off the ground, either by hanging the slaughtered animal up or working on it on a bench of some kind, on the animal's own skin, or on a bed of strewn vegetable matter (straw or leaves). Undoubtedly this should be seen as a practice whose symbolic content needs to be examined in greater detail.

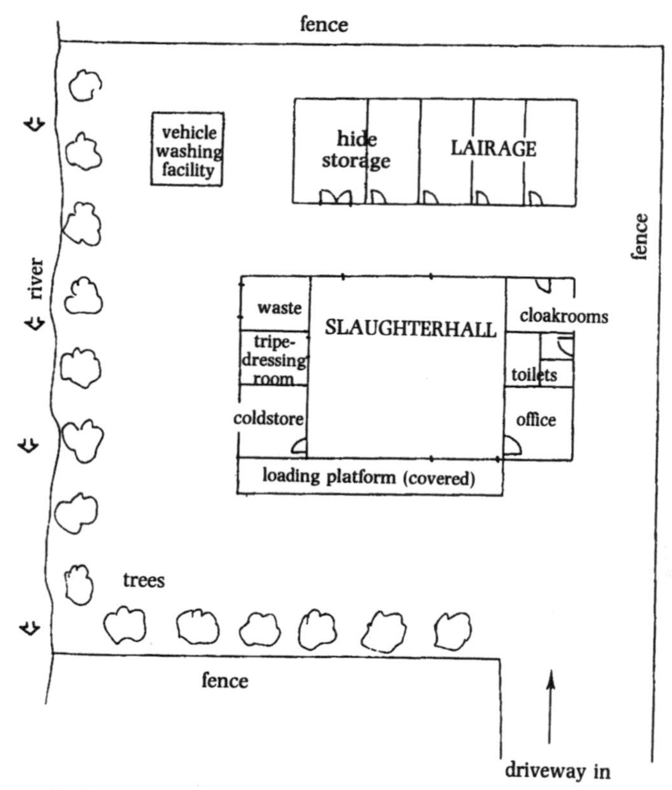

17 A small abattoir (fewer than 500 tonnes a year).

The 'clean' and 'dirty' sectors do not have separate entrances. Stunning and bleeding are not partitioned off from the slaughterhall.

Slaughter/dressing [*abattre/habiller*]

As the scene of the transformation of 'dirty' into 'clean', the slaughterhall is at the same time, inevitably, the place where those opposites meet, which is the thing most feared. The area contaminated by the contact may be circumscribed, but there is no avoiding it completely. Bluntly, slaughter may be confined to the slaughterhall, but someone still has to kill the animals. The attempt to resolve this problem proceeds by way of fresh fissions, and it becomes increasingly clear from this point on that such separations are in fact repetitions of the initial one. They go well beyond the purely technical imperative, producing a kind of secondary symbolic benefit.

The operations performed on an animal in the slaughterhall may be summed up in a few words. It will be successively:

18. *Breakdown of dressing of various species CEMAGREF, March 1982, 'Technical note: multi-use slaughter lines', p. 6*

Functions	Major operations	Remarks	
SLAUGHTER	– introduction		
	– containment	LB:	individual, with slump control devices
		C, O:	in batches
	– anaesthetisation	*methods most frequently used:*	
		LB:	trepanation
		YB, C:	percussion
		O:	electronarcosis
	– bleeding	LB:	prethoracic and/or jugulation
		YB:	jugulation
		C, O:	jugulation or throat-cutting
	– draining		
	– cutting-off of legs		
	– marking out		
	– flaying of front	*For flaying by hand*	
	– flaying of back	LB, C:	use of a tool
	– flaying of flanks	O:	flaying by manual 'punching'
	– flaying of back and removal of hide		
	– removal and processing of head	LB:	flaying, removal of tongue
		O:	flaying
		C:	evacuated in skin with tongue to tripe room
EVISCERATION	– opening-up		
	– splitting of chump end	LB and C only	
	– separation and washing of stomachs		
	– splitting of sternum	LB, C:	standard
		O:	optional
	– separation and washing of other viscera	LB:	liver separated
		C, O:	liver remains attached to lungs/heart/spleen complex
SPLITTING		LB only	
HYGIENE INSPECTION			
SUPPLEMENTARY OPERATIONS	– removal of kidneys and leaf fat	LB and C	
	– trimming		
	– trussing of forelegs	more standard with C and O than with LB	

LB: large bovines, including young bovines (YB), unless indicated otherwise, and horses; C: calves; O: ovines and caprines (sheep and goats).

immobilised, anaesthetised, suspended, and bled;
flayed (or scalded and dehaired in the case of pigs);

eviscerated;

sometimes split in two vertically (this operation is carried out on pigs and large bovines);

weighed (strictly speaking, this operation has nothing to do with slaughtering or slaughterers, even if it is materially associated with the slaughterhall).

The table reproduced in figure 18, which is taken from a study by the [French] national agricultural research body CEMAGREF [*Centre national du machinisme agricole, du Génie rurale, des Eaux et Forêts*, 'National centre for agricultural mechanisation, agricultural engineering, and rivers, lakes, and forests'], gives a clear analytical view of the operations involved. We shall return later and in more detail to the species-dependent variations. Here let us simply note that the table takes no account of pigs, being concerned only with 'butchery [*boucherie*] animals'. The exclusion is in line with custom (pork, in France, is traditionally the province of the *charcuterie* trade) and consistent with the report's intention, which is to examine the possibility and profitability of multi-use slaughter lines. The special treatment applied to pigs, at least as regards flaying, rules them out of a wholly multi-use approach.

All these operations constitute slaughtering in the broad sense. Strictly speaking, however, *abattage* refers only to the actual killing of animals. It is clearly, even physically, separate from the operations that follow.

The separation is of course justified on various practical grounds. The animals need to be penned or routed through a race in such a way that they cannot escape and may be approached and held conveniently and without risk. There is probably also some advantage in having the noise of the machines running inside the hall reduced somewhat (Bochet 1983, pp. 128–30; CEMAGREF 1982b). But above all it is a matter once again of separating clean from dirty. Even stunned, an animal being bled may continue to move for a few moments, scattering blood that hygiene requires shall not fall on carcasses already in the process of being flayed. Thus a partition or a chicane (or both) prevents such tainting and objectively tips the actual slaughter room over into the 'dirty' side of the abattoir or (worse) makes it the most ambiguous place in the slaughterhall.

The slaughter room is variously laid out, depending on the species dealt with. Figures 19 and 20 show examples of slaughter rooms encountered during the course of the study. The first thing to notice is that the stunning and bleeding of pigs are not isolated from the operations that follow. This is for technical reasons in that pigs' blood is collected and defibrinated in mechanical stirrers and their bodies are immediately immersed in a scalder. It is perhaps worth noting that the scalding machine is often sited in such a

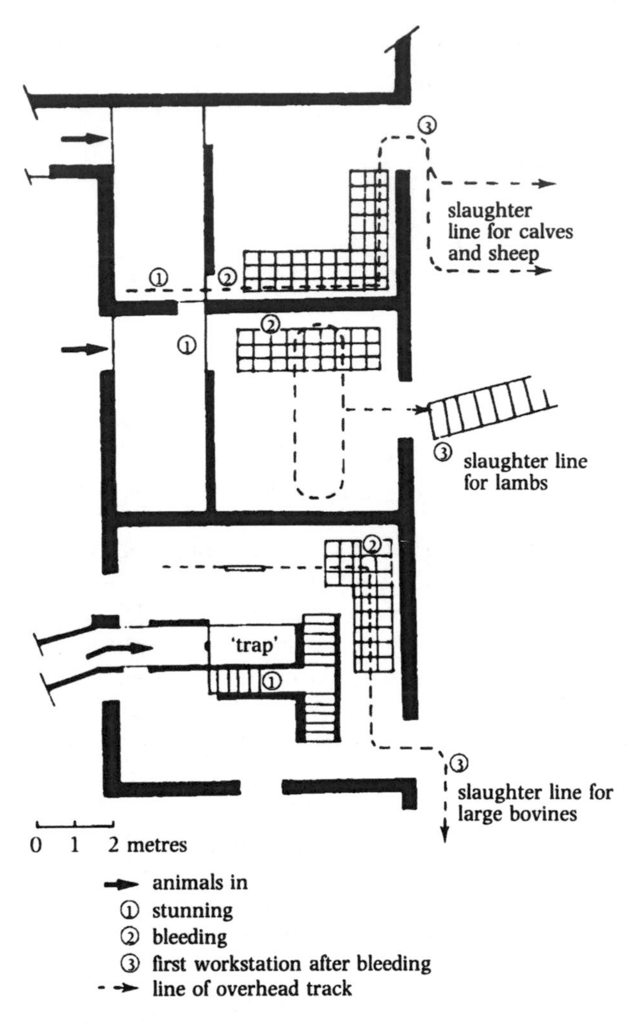

19 Abattoir layouts I

position that its bulk conceals the slaughter station from those working farther down the line (nearer the 'front'). However, this is not always so, and it is impossible to state that such is the intention. In some abattoirs, equipped with multi-use slaughter lines, pigs are slaughtered in the same room as calves and sheep.

The principal difference in the layout of slaughter rooms has to do with volume and with the strength of such animals as large bovines and horses. These need to be very firmly restrained, as much for the safety of the workers as, paradoxically, for their own safety (on which worker safety also depends). Large animals are brought from the lairage (or lorries) to the slaughter room

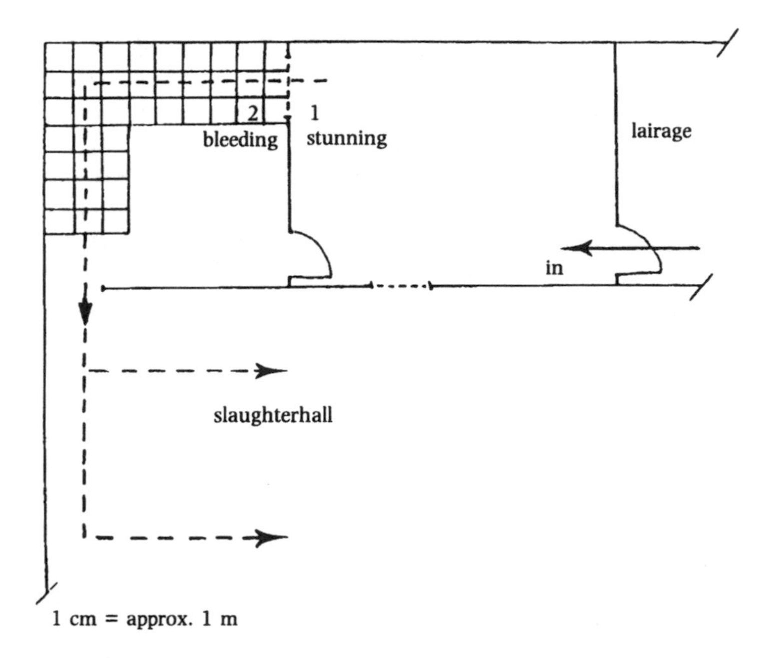

20 Abattoir layouts 2.

along a race [the 'stunning race'] between walls or tall barriers where they can only advance in single file. At the end of the race they enter what in technical parlance is a 'restraining pen' ['*box de contention*'] but French slaughtermen refer to as the 'trap'. The animal does indeed now find itself in a cul-de-sac: it can neither turn around nor escape, being as tightly contained as in the race but with its advance now cut off by a wall. A partition comes down behind it to separate it from the other animals. Standing on steps, a man will apply the stunning pistol to the animal's head, and then operate the mechanism that tips the stunned animal out of the 'trap' directly beneath the winch that will hoist it by one of its hind legs and hook it on to the overhead track. A few metres farther on it will be bled, while the next animal is being stunned.

Smaller animals do not require such firm restraint and will often be herded into a pen in batches to be stunned, calves with the stunning pistol, sheep and pigs with electrodes. A chain is passed around a hind leg, and the animal can then be hoisted up an elevator rail to the overhead track. However, abattoir refurbishment projects will gradually introduce the stunning race for all species, adapting it to their build. Such races already exist in abattoirs that specialise in handling a single species, particularly pigs. The quest for technical rationalisation and economic profitability may alter this or that detail, but the principle is still the same, namely to cut off the actual slaughter from the rest of the hall and to make people's jobs easier by reducing direct handling of livestock to the absolute minimum. The 'trap' system for larger animals may thus be regarded as exemplary, with other arrangements being explicitly defined as approximations to it.

In every case the physical separation from the rest of the hall is complete and consists in a wall rising all the way to the ceiling. This separation is reinforced by another, which may be either a second wall or a simple barrier. Finally, the overall layout is always such that the isolation has a twofold significance: it provides for the mutual invisibility of men, on the one hand, and animals, on the other, and hence of flaying and slaughtering, of the dying animal and the carcass, of the dealing of death and the inert object processed subsequently.

Everything is done as if the animal was not meant to see the place it is entering, as if it was entering nowhere. It does indeed enter an impasse. *Qua* animal, it has reached the end of the road. After this it will be something else, namely a carcass. And in physical terms its de-animalisation begins with suspension, as a result of which it ceases to have 'its feet on the ground'. Even when bleeding was not done in the hanging position but on the ground, the animal was immediately thrown on to its back [on a piece of apparatus called a '*guinchet*'] with all four hoofs in the air (an impossible position for a live animal), about a foot off the ground. Whichever procedure is adopted, the animal is no more, after being bled (and nowadays immediately after being stunned), than a substance to be processed. Between the moment of death and the final presentation of the carcass there is a nameless void: the object is neither an animal, not even (especially not even) a dead animal (a corpse, unfit for consumption), nor is it yet meat.

And just as the animals cannot see where they are entering, so the slaughterhall personnel are equally unable to see them coming, because of the wall. All they will see is the result of the stunning and bleeding, namely a bloodless and virtually inert body approaching them on an overhead rail. They will be able to process a 'something' that has emerged from 'nowhere'. Seen from the hall, the slaughtering takes place somewhere else.

Thanks to this strict separation between hall and slaughter room, it is just as if man and animal were respectively nothing to each other, hidden somewhere else and hence as if non-existent. The physical separation arising out of a concern for hygiene succeeds in separating man from animal even on the threshold of the slaughterhall. And inside the slaughterhall, animal is no more.

At the actual slaughter station, however, man and beast have to meet. At least one man must face the inevitable. In fact two do, which changes everything by introducing a fresh division.

Stunning/bleeding [*assommer/saigner*]

We know that stunning was traditionally practised only on the larger animals (bovines and equines, i.e., members of the horse family), and then more through concern for the safety of men than out of regard for the suffering of animals. Preliminary anaesthetisation is now compulsory by law, even for small livestock, and the legal obligation is respected because it is accompanied by penalties severe enough to be persuasive. We also know that such anaesthetisation was dictated by a concern to make our behaviour towards animals more humane. However, now that the law is in force and applied it has effects that were certainly never anticipated by those who inspired and those who passed the legislation.

Let us take a closer look at how an animal is slaughtered. Once it is in the 'trap', a first man stuns it and, alone or with the help of a second man, hangs it up. Then the helper (or a third man) proceeds to bleed it. We thus observe, in these decisive actions of the killing process, a supremely delicate dissociation between individual acts and between individual actors. Even if it does not seek and was not intended to create it, the legal obligation to practise preliminary anaesthetisation has in fact produced this dissociation between the shedding of blood and the administering of death.

Who kills the animal? The person who stuns it, or the person who bleeds it? Not only is such a doubt formally possible; it exists in reality. When asked, some will say that the bleeding alone causes death, which is true; but they will promptly add that, once stunned, the animal feels nothing: 'it's as if dead', and bleeding merely finishes off a death that would in any case not be long in coming. Others consider the stunning crucial, and the reason they give is *the same one*: 'it's as if dead' ['*il est comme mort*'], and what follows can no longer matter to it.

Contrary to appearances, what we have here is not a sequence of operations but a disjunction – and even a *double disjunction*: between bleeding and death on the one hand; between death and suffering on the other. Indeed, the first man does not really kill, he anaesthetises. The second (or third) does not really kill either; he bleeds an animal that is already inert and, in the terms that are in constant use, 'as if dead'. The result of dissociating death from suffering in this way is as follows: since anaesthesia is not really fatal and since painless (or supposedly painless) bleeding is not really killing, we are left without any 'real' killing at all, nor do we have any one person who 'really' kills; by separating the jobs, you completely dilute the responsibilities and any feelings of guilt, however vague and held in check.

There is an obvious analogy here with Greek sacrifice (as analysed in Durand 1977, pp. 46–61): once all the participants in the mythical foundation sacrifice have been judged, and all have cascaded their responsibility on to the next one down the line, it is the knife that is pronounced guilty and as such sent into exile (it was thrown into the sea). Each person sets out what his own action consisted in, and since no one can take upon himself what all did collectively, the knife is charged with the crime because it cannot speak. The guilty party is the one that cannot express what it has done, which is surely the best way there could be of saying that what has been accomplished is something unspeakable?

Closer to our own experience, there are other, similar cases of dilution among the many of the responsibilities of each. In a firing squad, at least one rifle is loaded with a blank, so that each person is able to believe, as he pulls the trigger, that he is not killing, or at least no one can be absolutely certain of having committed a fatal action. Likewise the sharing of disturbing jobs between a number of agents enables each of them to take refuge in ignorance of the whole action in which he is involved.

In the same way, in a place where animals are slaughtered each person is able to say what he does: one anaesthetises, the other bleeds. Two men are necessary for neither of them to be the real killer.[2] The double disjunction, by repeating the fatal moment, only evades it the more effectively. All that remains is the elusive residue of two distinct actions. Repetition (dividing the act in two) removes the decisive element; the action of each man is left indecisive; the key moment, the crucial point, is reduced to the harmless suspension of a body that had slumped to the floor.

'Killers'/slaughterers [*tueurs/abatteurs*]

The *Littré* dictionary, as we have seen (p. 30, above), said all there was to say: *abattre* means 'to bring down that which is standing'. Notice how the words have a precise meaning. Linguistic euphemism backs up a sort of practical euphemism. The technical and organisational aspects of the jobs and actions involved can function euphemistically just as much as the words. It is possible to avoid an act in the very moment of performing it, just as it is possible to avoid a meaning in the very moment of uttering it. All it takes is a sufficiently large incision in the continuum of reality and meaning.

In France, *tueries* have disappeared from the vocabulary (except for the purposes of referring to slaughterhouses in the past) and have been replaced by *abattoirs*, as those who work in them are no longer called *tueurs* but *abatteurs*. 'It's more humane,' people will tell you. Above all, as we have seen, it is more vegetable, evoking as it does the work of the woodcutter. A man who had in fact been a woodcutter before working as a slaughterman said how surprised he had been to find that he remained an '*abatteur*'.

2 The fact that staff shortages will occasionally dictate that one person does both jobs does not in essence alter anything. That person cannot deny that he is killing, but he is able to be ignorant of *when* he kills and, as he performs each function, to shift the decisive effect onto the other.

However, the latter term has not had the same fate as *abattoir*. Specialised documents of a technical or occupational nature occasionally employ the term *tueur*, and in the vast majority of cases the men concerned refer to themselves as *tueurs*. Clearly, use of the word in this instance is a transposition of terms from the *langue d'oc* and Basque dialects of this part of France. In those dialects, and in the rural circles in which they are spoken all the time, everybody knows what a *tueur* is; no further explanation is required. Familiarity with animals implies a clear distinction between them and people, between the normal fate of the one and of the other, and when someone uses the word *tueur* he can only be talking about animals. 'It's only countryfolk who have any respect for us,' you will often hear. Their level-headedness stems, of course, from their sense of gratitude for a skill they can call upon whenever a pig or a lamb needs to be slaughtered on the farm but also from the absence of ambiguous images associated with a word that literally means 'killer'. It is only very rarely, outside common usage and with the nature of the victims specified, that the local languages will use the term *tueur* metaphorically to refer to a murderer.

In French, on the other hand, the language of townsfolk who, people will say, have 'never seen an animal [meaning livestock] close to', *tueur* is offensive and immediately suggests the idea of murder. It expresses horror of a person who kills his own kind, while the killing of animals becomes burdened with disapproval even where it is acknowledged to be necessary. So the killing of animals had to be euphemised in order to distinguish it from the murder of men. It became *abattage* and was originally the job of *garçons d'abattoir*, who were in turn euphemised into *abatteurs*.

However, this appellation only seems to operate for external consumption, as it were. When addressing people who 'do not know', people for whom *tueur* has a pejorative connotation, you have to say (or write) *abatteur*, which has no such connotation. But inside an abattoir (and in the meat trade generally) it is obvious that being a *tueur* has nothing to do with being a murderer.

Vocabulary varies from situation to situation. Anyone who is familiar with the premises and/or the people who work there will say, like the latter, *tueur*. But outside that precisely delimited field, the term casts a chill, as the small boy discovered who, when asked at school what his father did, unleashed astonishment and hilarity by naively replying that he was a *tueur*, as he was used to doing. 'The children thought of the killers in westerns,' the boy's father commented, telling me the story. Adults automatically adapt their vocabulary to the person they are addressing. With me, for instance, people would use either term indiscriminately, the degree of naturalness with which they did so depending on how deeply they suspected me of adhering to received ideas; eventually, *tueur* was the only word they used. But what about strangers, people outside the abattoir, what do they say to them? What do they say to new friends, for example? The answer is that they usually resort to paraphrase ('I work at the abattoir'), though that is not always enough. The best solution is to call oneself a '*boucher*' [literally, 'butcher']: 'butcher is not the same, butcher's a trade'. The inference here is that *tueur* is not really a trade. Moreover, this is a distinction claimed by those of the *abatteurs* who really are *bouchers* or who are trained as such; they are very ready to look down on the others, in fact: 'they're *tueurs*, they don't know their meat or their animals' (in other words, they are ignorant regarding the quality of the product they help to process).

It is only by being recognised as a trade that slaughtering can in fact be practised. The only woman encountered thus far who had worked as an *abatteuse* (she is now retired) was quite explicit in her account: she 'got into it' by marrying a slaughterer at a time when 'you had to help your husband'. She went on:

My getting into it was because [her emphasis] *at any rate it didn't hurt the animals. Otherwise I shouldn't have done it. Oh, I couldn't stand that! . . . It's a trade, animals have to be slaughtered, it's a trade!*

This insistence on slaughtering being a trade may go so far as to reject its being bracketed with that of the butcher. Such was the case with the slaughterer who, on the day of the test for his CAP [*Certificat d'aptitude professionelle*], refused to cut up an animal: 'that's not my job. I'm a slaughterer, not a butcher [*je suis abatteur, pas boucher*].

What is certain, if we are to believe all the accounts, is that the golden age of the trade lies in the past. Job fragmentation on the slaughter line has seen to that.

2 I'VE ALWAYS LIKED IT'

'Why did you come into this job?'

'Because I've always liked it. The abattoir used to be not here but on the other road, over there, fifty yards from the school, and as soon as I came out of school, rather than get on with my homework, ma'am, I used to go to the abattoir. It's always been in my blood.'

'What was it you liked so much?'

'Everything, ma'am – killing, flaying, washing the entrails, all of it, ma'am, I enjoy the whole job from start to finish. And doing the markets the way we used to. Now they do one market a week, whereas before we used to drive around more, doing more markets. We used to slaughter calves, and when I got my driving licence, in the evening at . . . I say evening, it was morning really, midnight or two o'clock, we'd get up, load the calves into the lorries, and take them off to the abattoir in Bordeaux . . . That's why I'm tough with the staff, even though they're my sons, I'm tough with them, oh yes, because I had a hard time of it, I can tell you, I didn't have a penny, not even when I came out of the army . . . '

A fragmented job

Indeed, the system of separation of tasks that we have seen in operation up until the moment of death does not stop there. It applies equally (one might almost say, all the more) to the work of flaying and evisceration.

Both in technical parlance and in the vocabulary of everyday, this part of the job is called *habillage* [literally, 'dressing',* the term used in English abattoirs], and the slaughterman dresses *une carcasse*, not an animal, because as we have seen the animal disappears in the act of suspension. As used here, the term 'dressing' never ceases to surprise, since the process referred to bears more relation to undressing.

In fact, the term stems from a long tradition that modern usage has respected on this point, possibly because it already incorporates an analogy. It is thought to be borrowed from the vocabulary of the kitchen, and so it may be: '*Habiller*,' writes the author of a 'literary history' of gastronomy, 'means to prepare poultry or game or any kind of whole creature (fish or meat)' (Revel 1979, p. 118). So *habillage* is strictly speaking a preparation job in the kitchen, as distinct from *appareillage*, which refers to 'the art of blending a number of products'. Originally, however, it formed part of the vocabulary of the woodcutter (see Bloch and Wartburg 1932), where it meant 'to prepare a billet of wood' (*abillier*). One is hardly surprised to come across a further vegetalising image, because as we shall see later the process of vegetalisation seems to have been taken just about as far as possible.

So carcasses are dressed; that is to say, they are got ready to be cut up for wholesale or retail marketing. This job, which until quite recently was done by one man (and still is in small abattoirs), is fragmented on slaughter lines into something like ten or a dozen jobs, depending on the type of animal concerned and the rate of slaughter.

The fact is, not all animals will be dealt with on the one slaughter line. We have seen already that pigs require special treatment and special machines. But neither are the other species mixed up together. Usually there are three slaughter lines, adapted to the size of the animals handled, namely large (full-grown bovines and equines), medium (calves and sheep), and small (lambs). This separation is dictated by the height of the animals when suspended. The rear flaying platforms for large bovines need of course to be higher than those from which calves and sheep are flayed, whereas lambs can be flayed on cradles or on a conveyor belt. The equipment will vary on each line, depending on the flaying method employed. The hides of bovines are removed with a tool called a strimmer [*Perco* in French]; those of sheep

* Although French uses the word *habillage* in a number of commercial and industrial contexts. To take just a few examples, *habillage* refers to the pruning of trees, the assembly of watches, the labelling and sealing of bottles, the packaging and presentation of merchandise, and the lagging of pipework [Tr.].

21 The strimmer [*'le Perco'*]

[often referred to as 'pelts', in English] are first cut into with a knife and then parted from the flesh by 'punching' [*poussage*] with the fist or with the aid of machines. Some partially multi-use lines already exist, and these will certainly become more common. They are equipped with height-adjustable platforms and machines to pull off hides and pelts that can be used for all species. In any case, allocation of animals to different lines is done not in accordance with zoological species but by category, the categories being determined by technical constraints that have to take account of two parameters, namely the volume of the animal and the type of skin. Modernisation is concerned to make the method of flaying uniform (i.e., peeling for all species) and to replace fixed equipment deployed horizontally with equipment that is mobile in the vertical plane.

Every line, however, whether multi-use or not, is characterised by division of labour, with each person being assigned to a precise (fragmentary) operation that he performs on animal after animal as the carcasses file past in front of him. Flaying thus proceeds from the 'rear' towards the 'front' in a space that is oriented and differentially valued by a progressive separation of the dirty from the clean, right through to the ultimate refinement of the trimmed carcass. Here again, what may at first glance look like a sequence of operations is in a deeper sense a series of iterative disjunctions applied to a heterogeneous whole and brought to a halt by the achievement of a homogeneous substance called meat.

Meat can thus be defined at the end of the dressing process as the homogeneous substance, all of a piece, that results from the elimination of the animal parts, whether external or internal, that gave the former whole its visible autonomy (hide, head, feet) or were the secret source of its animation (heart, lungs, liver, guts). An animal (in the ordinary sense of an animated creature) is from the point of view of consumption simply a machine for manufacturing flesh; once the product has reached maturity and been harvested (or 'felled', one of the meanings of *abattage*), dressing releases the meat from its biological apparatus, the sole purpose of which was to secrete it. The whole dressing process is thus in fact an undressing, not only in that it removes the animal's external envelope but above all in that it strips the flesh of its animality, detaching the organic substance from its biological foundations: meat is an organic substance obtained by dispersal of the biological. As a result, if the butcher is subsequently able to distinguish cuts of different qualities (something that was not done before the eighteenth century), he is making decisions only about secondary properties, never about substances.

However, to separate the biological element from the edible flesh, it is necessary to enter into contact with what you are eliminating, and until the process is complete there is still some animal left in the carcass. It is a thought-provoking fact that the first industrial production lines were in fact slaughter lines in the Chicago abattoirs (Benoist 1980, p. 101; Léry 1971, p. 29; Miller 1962). We know the effects of job fragmentation in terms of lowering awareness levels, and its application to slaughtering is probably no accident. Each man is able, as he performs a task that has been reduced to a small number of movements, to overlook the significance of those movements. Slaughterers often stress that once you 'get used to it' you 'stop taking any notice', you 'do it as you would anything else'. The thought vacuum and the lack of identification with one's job that are elsewhere experienced as distressing features of production-line work, here constitute on the contrary a prerequisite for 'getting used to it'.

However, this reduction of awareness finds its limit in resistances within the material being processed. Job fragmentation is fully effective only in connection with material that is perfectly regular and always the same. Here, though, the regularity is only ever approximate; the suspended body retains traces of the unique life that once animated it: illnesses it may have had, accidents it may have suffered, various anomalies that may characterise it. The contingency and individuality of the biological sphere resist the formal rigour of technical organisation. So in addition to job fragmentation there will be another method of attempting to contain thought. This will be a normative judgement.

Hygiene inspection is the responsibility [in France] of *ad hoc* inspectors drawn from the veterinary services. But it is the slaughterers who are the first to see the carcasses they dress, and they quickly learn to assess how closely those carcasses conform to hygiene standards. They are further required to keep an eye on hygiene at work, ensuring that their tools, hands, clothes, etc. are clean. The animals' progress down the line is thus not entirely smooth but tends instead to be punctuated by minor incidents: a knife that needs sharpening, a tool that needs washing after contact with a diseased organ or escaped secretion, and so on. Thought is thereby directed towards the methods used to accomplish what is being done, towards the standards that must be maintained, and it fills, sometimes to ambiguous effect, the vacuums left by the way in which the job has been fragmented. Yet all the textbooks dealing with the training of slaughterers are consistently concerned to reinforce, at every opportunity, a kind of hygiene-conscious super-self, as if to harness thought to assessing the relationship (and filling the gap) between the resistant real and the sterilised ideal, thus curbing any possible drifts of meaning.

However, those same textbooks, like the professionals themselves (as well as slaughterers old enough to have known other working methods), all complain about the skill decline among slaughterers on lines. In principle, no one is attached to a particular workstation on a slaughter line, but in practice most workers are always assigned to the same jobs. Only a limited number are capable of working at several stations indiscriminately, and very few indeed are capable of dealing with a whole animal from start to finish. That kind of all-round skill is scarcely found any more except in small abattoirs where traditional methods are still in use.

The logic of the scissions that began with banishing abattoirs from towns is in fact taken to its conclusion only in large abattoirs (large in terms of volume of throughput), though there are many medium-sized establishments exhibiting every degree of partial modernisation. In other, even smaller abattoirs, which only have minimal equipment, the slaughterers still possess that skill inherited from the past, the gradual decline of which is so widely deplored.

3

FLAYING THE ANIMAL: THE PATIENT METAMORPHOSIS

A single space

Industrial abattoirs admit visitors. Usually these are people involved in the industry, coming to assess the advantages of this or that particular arrangement, but they will also occasionally be groups of schoolchildren, who may or may not be interested in the meat trade as a career.

If I may be permitted a parenthesis at this point, children do not, for the most part, react to the slaughter of animals with the terror one might expect. They are fascinated, in the main, as if by some mystery, or alternatively they tend to hoot with laughter. Georges Franju, talking about the public reception of his documentary film, *Le Sang des bêtes*, had this to say:

> It [the film] was scheduled for *Studio 28*, who never screened it because they were afraid to do so. Then it went to *Le Reflet* but was thought to be too violent and was pulled out after a couple of programmes. And then it was shown by mistake (by mistake!) at the Venice Festival, during a children's matinée. Apparently it had them all in stitches. I once showed the film myself to an organisation called the Young Animal-Lovers' Club. You should have heard them, they roared with laughter! The parents didn't laugh but the kids did. I mean, animals get slaughtered, right? It was a good giggle for them (from an interview broadcast by France-Culture, March 1985).

I never came across that kind of hilarity during abattoir visits, but no doubt the filmed quality even of so uncompromising a documentary as Franju's takes away something of the reality of what it shows precisely by amplifying it. Reality knows no close-ups, no editing, no commentary, no music, etc.

Visiting is possible, then, in industrial abattoirs. And if strict standards of hygiene demand that the guided tour should go from 'clean' to 'dirty' sectors, in fact it proceeds in the opposite direction; that is to say, it follows the order of the operations that turn animals into carcasses. To put it another way, the visitor's route parallels the one-way path of the animals. This direction is that of the technical organisation of operations; it is the only one, the visitor will be told, that makes it possible to 'understand properly'. The visitor need be only vaguely aware that his route is the one traced by the animals for this direction to be experienced as disturbing. However, seeing round an abattoir in the opposite direction would be like watching a film backwards; it would mean reconstituting the animal from the starting-point of the carcass, and that would be at least equally disturbing, since it is precisely what the repeated disjunctions seek to make impossible.

Visitors are not admitted to abattoirs dealing with small volumes of traffic. One reason, of course, is that there is nothing exemplary about them, but the chief reason is that no *tour* as such is possible. Granted, the visitor can see round the buildings, noting the layout of the various sheds, but once he reaches the slaughterhall, that is the end of the trip. There the whole spectacle confronts him; there he must stop and take the whole thing in as he sees, patiently deployed in time, the transformation of which, elsewhere, the individual moments are distributed in space. The overall scene is certainly a varied one, with a number of people working in the hall at the same time. But each person's job constitutes a distinct scene of its own, defined by the activity of one or two men around a flaying cradle or a suspended bullock; it has its own centre and its own rhythm, to which the observer must adjust.

Obviously, other things disappear too, namely the anxiety that may be occasioned by a sense of following parallel paths and above all the bewilderment provoked by the massive scale of industrial abattoirs, which one realises must have greatly influenced the layout of abattoirs dealing with large tonnages. It becomes clear that the logics appropriate to one layout or another stem neither from the same constraints nor from the same people.

Small abattoirs have no 'trap', nor do they have any way of containing animals. At most a few mobile barriers will be used to pen small livestock near the slaughterhall entrance, where a firm grip will briefly immobilise them for anaesthetisation. Large bovines are held with the aid of a long rope, one end of which is looped around the animal's horns or neck while the other end is passed through a ring set in the concrete floor. Traction on the rope will bring the animal's head down close to the ring. The animal and the man pulling on the rope are then in approximately the positions shown in the illustration from Diderot's *Encyclopédie* reproduced here as figure 22. However, the man doing the stunning no longer brandishes a poleaxe; he uses a humane killer called a 'captive-bolt pistol', applying it to the brow of the animal, which promptly slumps to the floor. In only one abattoir did I see the 'cane' ['*jonc*'; in English, 'pithing rod'] still in use; this is a long flexible stick introduced into the hole now perforating the animal's skull in such a way as to reach the spinal cord. The process is supposed to 'activate death' (Chaudieu 1970, p. 87) and bring about 'the complete annihilation of the animal' (Baillet 1880, p. 143). Not qualified to pronounce on this myself, I can only say that it does not make the death any less spectacular, exacerbating as it does the animal's final reflex movements.

Anyway, the animal is then hung up to be bled at a point right beside the ring in the floor and as close as possible to a drain grating, down which the

22 Plate from Diderot's *Encyclopédie ou Dictionnaire raisonné des sciences et des arts* (1751–72), article *Boucher*

blood disappears, assisted on its way by a jet of water. Dressing is usually done with the animal suspended in the same place or, if it is necessary to give the next animal time to bleed while the first is being flayed, a few metres farther on. The animal may also, after bleeding, be lowered on to a cradle to be flayed and then hung up again for evisceration.

Small livestock are always dressed on cradles, which the peeled-off hide covers like a tablecloth in such a way that the carcass never comes into contact with the cradle (see figure 61). The parts that have been removed (waste, offal, entrails, hides) fall to the floor or into various containers and are then transported to the nearby tripe-dressing room, hide store, or wastebins.

So horizontal flaying still exploits the vertical dimension for sorting purposes. Vertical industrial abattoirs may in fact be seen as an extension of that verticality. As such they seem closer to traditional methods than the more common type of industrial abattoir, in which separation of the various elements is done horizontally, exploiting the vertical dimension only in order to give runners and drainage channels the fall needed to take products away or to drop solid waste on to the floor, where it is collected in bins. Also in evidence is the way in which industrial abattoirs eliminate man-movements by using various architectural and technical devices, thus containing those who work in the slaughterhall even more rigorously.

In a small abattoir there is no job fragmentation in space and among workers. Inside a confined space a transformation is effected, each moment of which erases the one before as much as it affirms a continuity between the successive states. Of course, not all slaughterers are equally skilled and meticulous, but in many instances the terms of Gascar's description are still appropriate, when he talks of the painstaking, methodical labour that was capable of forcing animals out of their ill-fitting sheaths and bones out of their matrix of flesh, liberating entrails and judiciously parcelling out the muddled gift that was presented to us a moment ago in the form of a bullock (Gascar 1953, p. 52).

Slaughtering as a craft resolving enigmas by analysis ...

*'Faire une bête'**

At a simpler level, slaughterers will say that they 'do/make an animal' or that they 'kill an animal'. The two terms, *faire* and *tuer*, are used indiscriminately; they mean the same thing. Indeed, it follows naturally that one does not stop at depriving the animal of life [*tuer*]; dressing the carcass is also included. One mentions only the crucial action; the inevitable sequel goes without saying. 'Doing/making an animal', on the other hand, shifts the emphasis on to the work of dressing and makes no mention of the initial killing. Might we perhaps be permitted to take these ready-made expressions quite strictly and deduce from their interchangeability what logic naturally suggests, namely that the animal that is killed is not the same as the one that is 'done/made' – even if we are, of course, in practical terms talking about the same creature? The killed animal is destroyed by its killing; the animal that is done/made is

3 'THE FLANK'S THE BEST ONE'

'Which workstations do you prefer?'

'Oh, the flank's the best one, so they say.'

'Doing the flowers [faire les fleurs]*?'*

'That's right.'

'Why?'

'It's the easiest.'

'Without catching the hide?'

'Yes. I mean, once you know how to do it, you never catch it, virtually never.'

'And when a person's starting out at fourteen or fifteen?'

'You're trained on ... in the tripe-dressing room. Then you move up to flaying, doing what we call cow collars, the neck and shoulders, because there's less risk of messing up the hides, its easier. And lastly flanks, that's easier to do, that's the neatest job.'

'The neatest job. But is it really easier?'

'Yes, that too.'

'Yet they make you do it last?'

'Well, of course, that's exactly why. Because everything's been freed, the top's been freed, the bottom's been freed ...'

'But it's what they teach you last?'

'Right, because usually, you see, the fellows who are there aren't in too much of a hurry to move over! They'll make way for you when they're on holiday, that's about it.'

* 'Doing an animal', yes, but the French word *faire* (from the Latin *facere*) simultaneously conveys the sense of 'make' or 'fabricate'. To keep this double reference present to the English reader, *faire* is here rendered by 'do/make' [Tr.].'

as if created from nothing, through the actions that constitute dressing, for use as food.

On the job, the word *tuer* may be confined to its narrower sense of simply killing. For instance, a man may ask an employee to help him kill an animal and then go back to his normal occupation. '*Faire une bête*', on the other hand, invariably denotes *all* the operations of slaughtering from killing to the final trimming; it means in fact to produce a carcass. And the decline of skills in industrial abattoirs is deplored in the same terms: 'they don't know how to do/make an animal any more', they only know how to perform part of the operation, but that does not do/make an animal! At best 'they' may be able to help out in an emergency, though not perhaps doing a particularly 'good job'.

So how does 'doing/making an animal' differ so greatly from the work performed on slaughter lines?

The first difference is that it is one man that 'does/makes an animal'. In fact it often takes two, particularly to flay a large bovine, but both have the knowledge and if necessary the ability to work alone.

The second difference is that the *bête* in the expression '*faire une bête*' is implicitly a large bovine, in the same way as, in Marie-Claude Pingaud's classic study of the people of Minot in Burgundy, *bêtes* are always cows (Pingaud 1978, p. 182). If a person knows how to kill and dress[1] pigs, no one will say that he knows how to do/make an animal; he merely knows how to 'kill pigs' ['*tuer les cochons*']. Nor if a person knows how to kill and flay sheep will anyone say that he can do/make an animal. The gap narrows when it comes to the skill involved in dealing with calves, which differ from large bovines only in size; here the point will be discussed as to whether the person in question 'could' in fact 'do/make an animal'. On the other hand, a person possessed of this supreme knowledge is *a fortiori* capable of doing/making a calf, though not necessarily all the other animals (he will have little liking for dealing with sheep and even less for dealing with pigs). Use of the expression *faire une bête* thus implies two parallel hierarchies (one of men, one of animals), a point to which we shall be returning in chapter 5.

The third difference is that 'doing/making an animal' implies a value judgement: it means doing it within the rules of the art. Not that industrial slaughtering is uniformly and necessarily botched, but it does not indulge in gratuitous refinements; it confines itself to respecting the demands of hygiene. The rules of the art require that care should be taken over the presentation of carcasses and that a person should work with sufficient skill not to become covered in blood immediately. The supreme skill is summed up in the stereotyped formula 'doing/making an animal in shiny shoes', which of course

[1] In fact the word *habiller* is rarely applied to pigs, which are not flayed. A key element in 'dressing', as we have seen, is the removal of the hide.

represents an ideal rather than a reality and above all expresses a desire on the part of the speaker to distance himself from the image of the brutal, blood-stained killer. Technical skill here goes hand-in-hand with cleanliness and moral dignity; it shows on the man as much as on the material he is processing.

The fact is, that process is not limited to producing something useful; it also seeks to produce something that 'looks nice', to decorate carcasses 'for show'. In the words of the *Encyclopaedia Britannica*:

> Butchers in slaughterhouses were at one time very highly trained craftsmen who efficiently and with some artistry conducted all the dressing operations on a carcass. [*Note, incidentally (though without reading too much into it), that such efficiency and artistry earn the name of 'butchers' for people who, without it, are simply 'men' at work.*] Today, with the moving chain conveyor operation, the dressing of a carcass has been separated into a number of simple, easily learned functions which are divided among a number of men, each doing his small specialized part (Miller 1962).

This artistic finishing, which only the really skilful know how to do, consists in using the knife in such a way as to give carcasses an appearance of having been sculpted. Naturally, it assumes its full dimensions when practised on *bêtes* proper (large bovines) or calves, in other words on noble material. This aesthetic concern serves to enhance natural shapes and qualities. No one is going to waste his time and talent on skinny, aged, sick, or otherwise inferior specimens. But on a fine animal the skilled slaughterman will know how to 'glaze' [*glacer*] the shoulders and thighs (i.e., leave a white, pearly film on the flesh), to split the spinal column with cleaver and knife in such a way as to leave the apophyses alternately to right and left, and finally 'to make flowers' or simply 'to flower' [*'faire des fleurs'*, *'fleurer'*], which means to remove the hide by making small incisions in the platysma or skin muscle (this is on the flanks only) in such a way as to obtain an abstract design not unlike, say, the raked sand of a Zen garden (Barthes 1970, pp. 102–3; see figures 23–4). This finish may be further decorated with 'palm-leaf' incisions fringing the ventral opening made for evisceration.

Decoration of meat could be taken to great lengths, as in the traditional Easter displays that celebrated the end of the meatless fast. From at least the end of the Middle Ages onwards it was customary to adorn the cuts of meat displayed for customers with plant material (Sébillot [1894] 1981, p. 106). While this tradition is still perpetuated (albeit with artificial greenery), gone are the days when carcasses were literally tattooed or coloured with actual blood and carefully arranged in compositions spilling out into the street in order to show off the butcher's skill even more than to attract customers. Probably such spectacles of fleshly abundance would not in fact attract anyone in an age where some butcher's shops no longer put meat out at all, preferring to cultivate the disinfected cleanliness of doctors' waiting rooms.

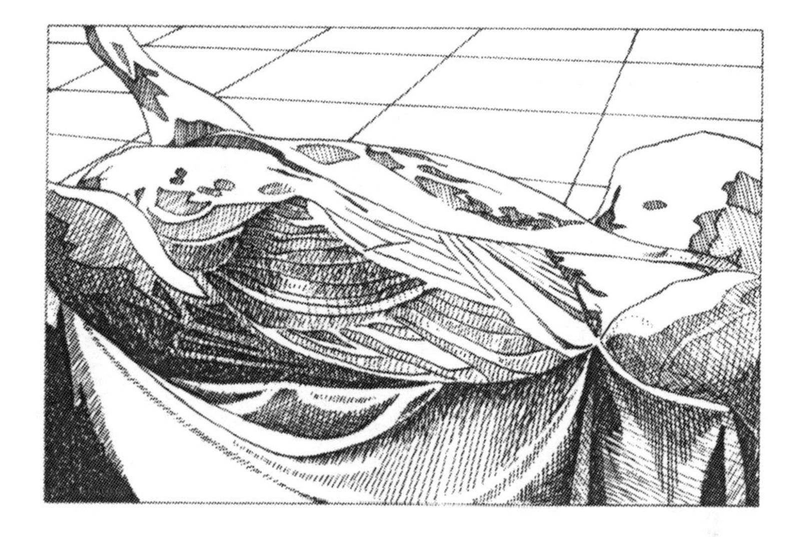

Carcass of a horse

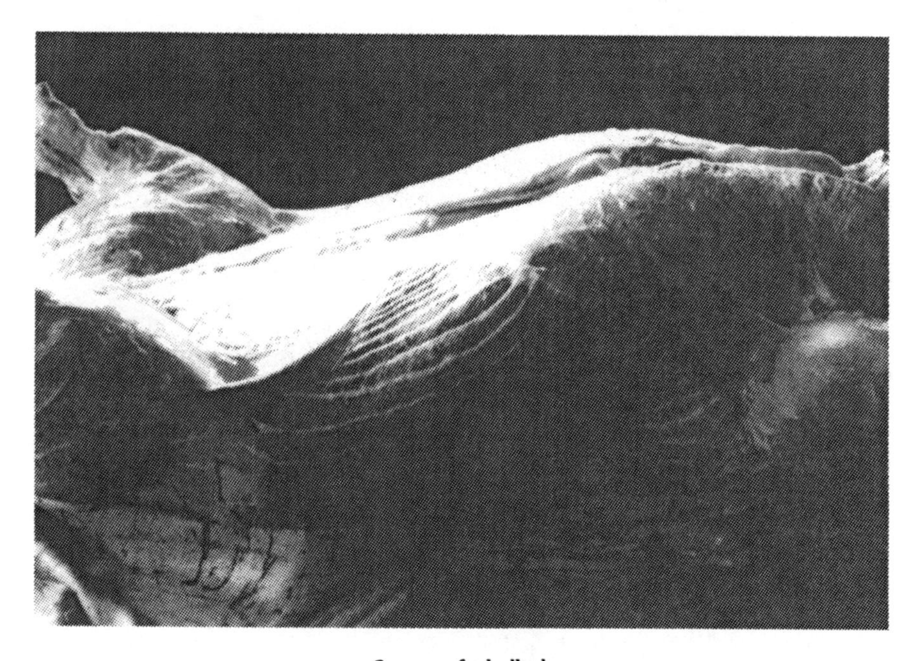

Carcass of a bullock

23 Two 'flowered' carcasses

24 'Flowered' veal carcasses.

Clearly 'flowering' may be practised to a greater or lesser extent. 'Palm leaves' is the name given to the incisions that decorate the muscle joining thigh (glazed) to flank ('flowered')

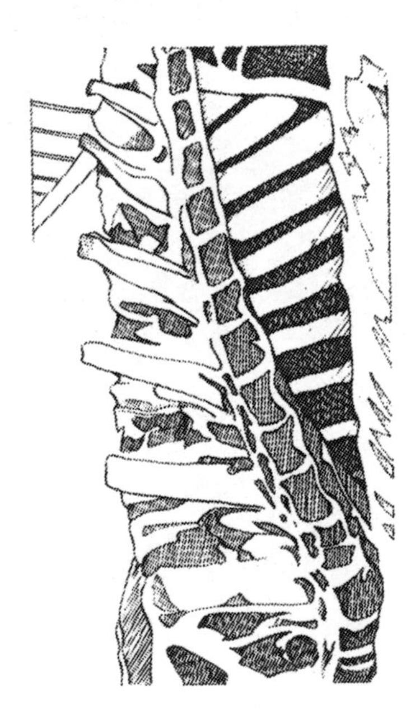

25 Split beef carcass

Such great displays (see figure 26) are no longer staged, so the embellishment of carcasses no longer serves a commercial purpose in anyone's eyes – with the exception, probably, of wholesalers. Indeed, even in an industrial abattoir it may sometimes happen that particularly well formed animals are 'flowered' as they always used to be, provided that there is someone on the staff capable of doing it. Their commercial value will certainly not be diminished thereby. However, in small abattoirs the essential motivation is still 'presentation' (still in demand from certain butchers), the pleasure of seeing and even of producing a fine carcass, of 'doing a good job' regardless of any more tangible benefit.

De-animalising

One recognises in all this, of course, the traditional values of the craftsman, the desire to 'do a good job' in which the workman's identification with his work found expression. In butchery, as in any other craft, creating a masterpiece (dressing or 'doing/making' a calf or bullock) was a condition of access to the rank of master, and as recently as the 1960s flaying championships were still held at regional and national level, leading to awards that were valued more for the honour they conferred than for any material gain.

Probably this should be seen in the same terms as any other kind of technical mastery, namely as a symbolic appropriation of matter; however, the precise forms it takes cannot possibly be arbitrary. The kind of matter that is processed in the slaughterhall of an abattoir is particularly loaded with a proliferation of meanings in urgent need of containment. Just as job fragmentation seeks to do in modern abattoirs, though using different procedures, the tradition of decoration in butchery seeks to check these vagaries of meaning. It does this by, so far as possible, sublimating the problem of the body.

To aestheticise is 'to wrest nature from its nature', 'to artialise' the raw fact (Roger 1978), in other words to substitute artifice, the human order, for the natural order. We know this at least since Hegelian aesthetics or since Baudelaire and in anthropology since Lévi-Strauss's analysis of Mbaya tattoos. The 'sublime distortion of nature' (Baudelaire's '*déformation sublime de la nature*') is peculiar to man, being the distinctive feature of thought in its deepest logic.

Here it takes the form it always assumes when applied to the body (Lévi-Strauss 1955, ch. 20, p. 215; Maertens 1978a, 1978b; Roger 1978, ch. 3, '*Pulchritudo adhaerens*'), namely that of 'adherent beauty', adherent to the point of being inlaid in the flesh (which is why tattooing offers the perfect example). 'Flowering' and the techniques of 'glazing' and modelling shapes do indeed constitute the 'making' part of 'doing/making an animal', i.e., a quite different animal from the one that walked in. They mean replacing the

26 Mr Viaud and his staff, around 1910 (from Gascar 1973, pp. 118–19; photo Harlingue-Viollet)

COIFFEUR

natural animal by a human creation, a process amounting to a veritable redemption of the natural fact by the rules of art or, if you prefer, a sublimation, whether this is understood in the alchemical or the psychoanalytical sense.

The fact that aestheticisation consists in taking possession of (in the double sense of rendering peculiar to man and making one's own) the animal that one 'does/makes' is inversely confirmed by the way in which meat considered unfit for human consumption is made to look repulsive (see above, p. 34). The method used is at the same time the token of that unfitness, and it has to do with appearance. It is in fact an anti-aestheticisation.

In this aestheticisation, this embellishment of carcasses, we find an extension of the vegetalising metaphor that originated with the terms *abattage* [which can also, remember, denote (tree-)felling] and *habillage* [from the forestry term *abilliage*]. Tracing an abstract design that has nothing floral about it, a man will nevertheless say that he is 'making flowers', as if every time we wish to euphemise the preparation of animals for the butcher's shop we are driven to borrow from the vocabulary of the vegetable kingdom, particularly as it relates to wood and greenery. Given the present state of our knowledge, it is very hard to explain this drive satisfactorily.

Clearly this de-animalising of meat as food constitutes an attempt to justify it, to bring the slaughter of animals into line with the felling of trees and the carnivorous into line with the vegetarian regime, to edulcorate blood into sap. One thinks, too, of the many traditions associating sage with pork, traditions found as far apart as Provence (Barrau 1983, p. 148) and Flanders (Messiant 1983, p. 222), as well as of those claiming that greenery wards off evil spirits (Sébillot [1904] 1984, p. 193), or referring to certain aromatic plants as 'herbs of death' (*ibid.*, p. 185). The vegetalisation of the death of animals can thus be situated within a whole complex of practices associating plants with funerary rites and beliefs, but the complex itself has yet to be explained. Going out on something of a hypothetical limb, one might also think of the permanence of the vegetable kingdom as supplying an adequate denial of the corruptibility and death of individual animate beings or alternatively that plant matter offers a good image of the de-individuation required to turn a living creature into something that may be eaten.

Finally, one thinks of the culinary practices that, still today, associate meat-eating closely with the consumption of vegetables. Meat and vegetables together form an almost ritual component of our menus, and traditional recipes (usually attributed to 'grandmother') have meat and vegetables simmering at length in creamy blends of one another's juices as if to effect an osmosis among the various ingredients and so temper the 'strength' and heat of meat with the gentle freshness of herbs and vegetables. It is the kind of cooking that has been characterised as 'well-tempered smoothness' (Zimmermann 1982, p. 198), both as to the body and as to the food.

All these approaches set the vegetalisation of carcasses in wider schemes of representation, yet they do little to explain it. We must be content simply to note that everything suggests that meat as food is accessible (or acceptable) only through the medium of the vegetable, which however one looks at it always comes down to de-animalising animals in order to take possession of their flesh.

Two logics, two moralities

However, such de-animalisation proceeds in a different manner in an industrial abattoir than in a small-scale establishment. In the latter context it operates at a material, manual level without any clear prior intention or reflection; in the former it is confined to the linguistic sphere and persists in the form of weary euphemisms, while the practical sphere has other avenues at its disposal, namely the iterative disjunctions that we have touched on already. This difference in procedural terms stems from different approaches.

The logic of industrial production initially conceives its solutions in accordance with a prior theoretical knowledge of the constraints of reality and of the objectives to be pursued; experts are consulted, of course, but not the men most directly confronted with the actual tasks of slaughtering. Those solutions then find expression in directives that in most cases take the form of standard requirements accompanied by penalties for non-observance. This is not only indicative of the ever-increasing hold exercised by the public authorities over a 'political commodity'; it also reveals a gap, which such requirements seek to close, between the experience born of practice and demands external to the trade.

This can be seen very clearly from the fact that technical planning is first of all done 'on paper'. *Abattoirs* are designed down to the last detail before they are built, which was obviously not the case with the *tueries* of a former age. The mere fact of drawing up plans involves a spatial projection of the temporal sequence of operations. A plan involves endless division, in fact, and the expression of that division in standards. It is thus the expression of a logic that, while systematic, is certainly less rigorously rational than appears at first sight. In fact, such prior representation of constraints and objectives is not impervious to shared representations concerning the death of animals, nor is it proof against the kind of sensitivity that renders that death suspect in our eyes, albeit without making vegetarians of us. The people who design the organisation of industrial abattoirs are well upstream in relation to the job of which they are defining the ways and means. In their everyday capacity as consumers, however, they are well downstream in relation to that same job and share the general view of slaughtering. As a result, the logic of the industrial abattoir not only satisfies the specific techno-economic demands of the industry concerned; it also satisfies the demands of modern sensitivities in that it meets and readily takes account of considerations relating to the humane treatment of animals as well as our obscure desire for our meat to be obtained without bloodshed, for slaughtermen to be 'just like other workers' and for abattoirs to be 'just like other factories'. Productivity, ordinariness, asepsis, and humaneness make a very effective combination here, as the remarks of one trainee abattoir manager showed beyond any doubt at all: an abattoir, he felt, should be as clean as a laboratory or operating theatre and so ordinary that nothing in it catches the eye. This is gradually coming to be the case, and in the abattoirs that conform most closely to modern standards people will express polite surprise at the ethnologist's interest. 'But there's nothing to see here,' they will say, and equally 'we've nothing to hide' (the two meaning the same thing). If everything is up to standard, there is nothing to be seen any more; indeed, the effect of standards and of conformity to standards is to render invisible what used to be a bloody spectacle. At the same time the colour of blood has been everywhere ousted by white: white walls, white accessories, white clothing from head to foot.

This logic of an external, explicit, normative asepsis making everything commonplace forms the basis of a code in hygiene: an obvious, easily verified cleanliness of persons, equipment, and premises is the outward and visible sign of a conformity to standards through which men can recover the kind of dignity that in the past was conferred on them by their skill. The requirement to 'be presentable' does not concern appearance alone; it signifies *normalcy* in every sense of the word. It also indicates that the 'presentation' of men and premises has replaced the aestheticisation we have just been looking at, which was also concerned with 'presentation', though of carcasses. If anyone ever doubted the fact, it is clear from this that the effect of appearances is never without significance.

The logic of the craftsman (in other words, of the man doing the job) inevitably proceeds otherwise. It is in tangible confrontation with matter that it finds its solutions, one by one, with no explicit prior plan. This does not indicate any passive, impotent mental inertia. A craft targets goals and passes on things learned, which may represent forces of relative inertia. However, not being guided by representations external to its own requirements, it produces a logic that is both less overtly systematic and less receptive to influences that have nothing to do with how it is done. That logic leads to an aesthetic code for which self-respect is achieved through 'a job well done', through the care put into 'presentation' of the result. Unable to escape the necessity of a bloody occupation, at least the man performing it does not reduce himself to its level but rises above it by asserting a skill that redeems both the initial act and its outcome.

A good illustration of the differences between these two logics may be found in the ways in which they diverge on the subject of stunning prior to bleeding. Compulsory anaesthetisation of all livestock slaughtered in abattoirs was introduced in 1964. Before that, only large bovines were stunned prior to bleeding, the safety of workers not requiring that small livestock be given the same treatment.[2] The absence of stunning was not – and is very often still not (even where stunning, being compulsory, is practised) – regarded as cruel; confidently and quickly performed, bleeding was considered to be as compassionate to animals as stunning, which was not referred to as 'anaesthetisation' and was not performed for any 'humane' reasons (unless, of course, the humanity was towards man).

Nor in any case can anyone be sure that such anaesthetisation, while it may *render* the animal insensible, is painless *in itself*. Vets differ on the subject. This is a good opportunity, in fact, to look at what they have to say, even if it means something of a digression.

The opinions reproduced here come from the same document, a technical manual published by the veterinary department of the [French] Ministry of Agriculture in 1974. In a passage dealing with standards for the slaughter of large animals, we read:

> For humane reasons the law requires prior stunning of all animals to be butchered, except those destined for consumption by the members of certain religions ... Defenders of this method of ritual slaughter will state, all considerations of religious belief aside, that it allows a very much better bleeding, which is plausible as well as promoting hygiene, but also that the procedure is humane and even preferable to stunning in this respect. They say that the abrupt fall in the blood pressure in the brain ensures an immediate loss of consciousness as surely if not more so than the traumatic method. The little that is known on the subject would seem to indicate that everyone is right and that, if we are rigorously objective, no problem arises. In fact, the spectacle of animals with their throats cut apparently still alive, thrashing about and splashing blood all over the place, is somewhat repugnant and one not easily borne. The requirements of decency alone justify the practice being prohibited. However, objective reason explains how in specific circumstances it is tolerated (Aufrant *et al.*, 1974, p. 54).

Farther on, in a discussion of the rules governing the slaughter of small livestock, we clearly have a different person writing:

> The inspector's job is to control the humaneness of the killing. The pistols of various kinds that provoke a violent but certain loss of consciousness, as does carbon dioxide, in connection with which we can truly speak of anaesthesia, leave little room for doubt. Where questions may be asked is in connection with electrocution, where it is not impossible that there is a period of conscious pain and where there is certainly a risk of failure. This is a thorny problem, being a difficult one to deal with calmly and objectively. Public opinion, including that of militant animal lovers, is by no means free of anthropomorphism and is readily deceived by appearances. Nothing will ever prevent people from thinking that animals 'feel their death', that the slitting of a

[2] The fact that kosher slaughtering makes it obligatory not to anaesthetise before bleeding would seem to confirm that the stunning of large livestock has to do with practical considerations (it takes a religious ban to stop people doing it).

sheep's throat is painful because ugly to watch, while an electric shock, on the other hand, is not, being clean, modern, bloodless, and obviously instantaneous (*ibid.*, p. 67).

The same author concludes that the best solution at all events is to give the job of stunning animals to 'workers with steady nerves and if possible a sincere desire to avoid causing the animals any suffering' while waiting for an advance that is 'bound to come' and to be 'more affordable than carbon dioxide equipment'.

Both texts merit detailed analysis. We shall be coming back to them, particularly as regards the clash (to which they both allude) between the 'rigorously objective' viewpoint and 'spectacle' or 'appearances'. For the moment we need only remark, on the one hand, that not all methods of anaesthetisation are absolutely certain and, on the other, that direct bleeding 'ensures an immediate loss of consciousness as surely if not more so than the traumatic method', so that 'everyone is right'.

Compulsory anaesthetisation, which became general at the time of the major reorganisation of the French abattoir industry in the mid 1960s, appears as the kind of standardisation that, through a dynamism of its own, imposes itself on the whole of the sphere in which its scope was originally limited. This extension of the authority of the rule was made easier by the fact that it was able to draw support from the humane concern to protect animals, which flowed from a representation of animate creatures that was not the one held by either stockbreeders or slaughterers.[3] Not that the latter had no regard for animal suffering, but their attentions were without 'humane' motivation and had never been theorised. We know, incidentally, that love of animals takes various forms and is quite capable of being present in those who kill them, be they hunters, butchers, or farmers. We have all, at one time or another, heard some story like that of the shepherd who preferred to kill his favourite lamb himself on the grounds that anyone else 'would hurt

[3] It should be added, for the sake of completeness, that humane motives are themselves reinforced by considerations of economy and hygiene. Thus a document dealing with the handling and housing of livestock at abattoirs concludes with the words: 'Well designed lairage makes it possible to provide the abattoir management with an effective instrument, the staff with a safer and more pleasant environment in which to work, and the animals with less distressing conditions of slaughter. A further interest (not a negligible one, either, despite its being less directly observable) is an improvement in the quality of the meat, because the final handling prior to slaughter affects that quality in ways that sometimes do not become apparent until the moment when the meat is carved, although their economic and hygienic importance is now well known' (CEMAGREF 1982b, p. 91). In fact, 'all these observations should be taken into account in order to reduce the suffering inflicted on the animals and its consequences as regards the quality of the meat' (*ibid.*, p. 99). One might perhaps look with a certain scepticism on this happy coincidence and ask how much weight humane motives would carry if they were incompatible with meat quality (commercial and gastronomic). However, what is more important (if also more disturbing) is the discovery that good treatment makes for good food.

it'. I have this example not from the shepherd himself but from a Franciscan monk, but I did occasionally overhear the kind of affectionate language that people normally use towards pets employed with the same naturalness to address the livestock that the speaker was engaged in slaughtering.

Traditional slaughtering did not feel that it was any more cruel to bleed animals without anaesthetising them than when it stunned them first, and as we have seen it may well have been right. The absence of stunning, where it did not serve a purpose in terms of worker safety, indicates that slaughtering was regarded as self-evidently necessary and was consequently done quite straightforwardly, without beating about the bush. By contrast, the transformation of the animal into meat, which was the condition of its access to the human table, formed the object of every sort of care. Bound up with human consumption, the embellishment of carcasses had nothing to do with any belated homage to the animals, even if it did highlight their natural qualities; it was qualities of meat, not of animality, that were exalted in this way.

Clearly, then, the logic of the job, the internal, implicit logic of the craftsman, is more regulatory than strictly normative. By offering a kind of anaesthetised ideal, it enables people to come to terms with reality; it also resists the anonymity imposed by large-scale slaughtering in that it individualises the substance processed. The craftsman, too, deanimalises carcasses but does so by quite different means than those employed in industrial production. However, the logic of the craftsman has ceased to exist (at least in the region studied here) except in the smallest abattoirs.

A recent skill?

Here as elsewhere industrial production has changed traditional practice and substituted its own laws for the values of the craftsman. However, before striking up a lament for the passing of 'a job well done', we ought in this case to check whether it really is ancestral know-how that is disappearing.

Since when have carcasses been 'flowered'? No author mentions the first appearance of the custom. My fieldwork provided no precise information

4 'I REALLY LIKE LIVESTOCK

'Let me tell you something. I'm a butcher, right? I slaughter livestock. But if I'd had the lolly I'd have bought land to put livestock on. See the difference? I like it, you see, I really like livestock, and yet I slaughter it. It's my trade, I like it. But if I'd had any money I'd have bought land to raise livestock. Because I'd have enjoyed seeing the stock in the field.'

'What kind of livestock?'

'Just livestock, cows. Looking after them, doing like they do nowadays, leaving them all outside, just that.'

here. Chaudieu's 'Little Dictionary of Butchery and Pork Butchery' defines *fleurage* in the imperfect tense on the grounds that it was practised 'before the use of flaying appliances' (Chaudieu 1970, p. 107). However, the said appliances (the tool referred to as a strimmer; see figure 21) were not the reason why *fleurage* went out, because when it is still practised nowadays it is more often done with the strimmer than with a knife. A knife (specifically the small one known as a '*lancette*' [lancet] that was used for flowering) may have enabled the butcher to do finer work, but use of the strimmer has not made *fleurage* impossible.

If we cannot discover for certain how old the practice is, we can nevertheless hazard a couple of hypotheses.

It might be thought that this was a very ancient custom. Indeed, we know (Elias 1939; Ketcham Wheaton 1983; Revel 1979) that at least until the seventeenth century huge pieces of meat, whole animals sometimes, were brought to the table and offered up to the skill of the carver, who had the honour of distributing to each person present the piece that befitted his or her rank. It might therefore be supposed that the animals concerned were flayed with care and skilfully 'dressed' right from slaughter.

However, the opposite hypóthesis may also be advanced, namely that this kind of aestheticised dressing appeared relatively recently. Because we also know that distinct cuts and joints did not appear before the eighteenth century (Gascar 1973, p. 46) and that for a long time they retained the peculiarities of regional custom; only gradually did the 'Parisian' cut gain acceptance among provincial butchers, and it never did so uniformly. The fact is that the appearance of the art of butchery coincided with the disappearance of that of the 'esquire trenchant'.

> Whereas the original norm regarded the sight of a slaughtered animal and its being cut up at table as a pleasant or at least by no means unpleasant one, things moved in the direction of a different norm, which postulated that it should so far as possible be forgotten that a plate of meat bore any relationship to a dead animal ... Cutting a carcass into pieces could not be abolished as such because it had to be done if the animal was to be eaten. But any *offence to sensibilities* was now relegated to a position *behind the scenes* [*author's emphasis*], well away from social life. It was henceforth done by experts in the shop or in the kitchen (Elias 1939).

Among those 'experts' were the butchers who officiated 'in the shop'. When the butcher cut up carcasses 'behind the scenes', he was doing to raw meat what the carver had done on the table to cooked meat. And it was at that point that the butchery trade learned to distinguish cuts of different qualities, thus effecting a social as well as a culinary distribution of the various parts of the carcass. The sequence of the persons qualified to cut up meat would thus be: nobleman, 'ecuyer trenchant', butcher. However, before abattoirs were sent into exile butchers used to slaughter animals themselves. This gives the art of 'presenting' carcasses as much a social as a symbolic

27 Ceremonial carving of the roast beef (from *Le Journal des voyages*, 1894)

significance, and it means that it is relatively recent – corresponding to the first 'shift behind the scenes' (Elias 1939) of the cutting up of carcasses, to an increase in the consumption of meat, and to an initial devaluation of its production. In other words, the banishment of abattoirs and the aestheticisation of carcasses occurred at more or less the same time, coinciding with the shift in sensibilities as a result of which people no longer wished either to witness slaughtering or to acknowledge that meat 'bore any relationship to a dead animal'. This second hypothesis seems more satisfactory than the first in that it demonstrates the link between social conditions and a symbolic activity. Indeed, if the symbolic field can always be analysed as autonomous purely within its own inner logic, it is never cut off from the social conditions that produce it or that enable it to function effectively.

Finally, this latter hypothesis would explain why it is that the aestheticisation of carcasses and the compulsive job fragmentation that characterises the industrial abattoir conspire towards the same end. They both stem from the henceforth pressing need increasingly to de-animalise the flesh we eat. Increased consumption draws large quantities of animals to the abattoir, and whereas the slaughter of a few animals may be a festive occasion, slaughter on a large scale is different. It is disturbing, therefore means must be found of putting it out of mind. Such means may range from the artisanal to the industrial, but the end is the same.

4

THE SHEDDING OF BLOOD

Bloodless flesh

Bleeding an edible animal is often a deliberate act of 'de-animation' of the meat to be eaten, having due regard to the strict etymology of the term, which comes from the Latin *anima* or 'breath of life' (Barrau 1983, p. 159)

To bleed an animal is indeed to take away lifc itself, the vital principle, therefore to de-animate. As such it is an inevitably radical act, allowing of no degrees, and it is what makes the subsequent transformations possible. For those transformations we might reserve the less radical term 'de-animalisation', for they do not in fact concern the vital *principle* but rather the bodily *form* of the animal, re-forming it and thus turning it into something edible, something quite different from a living body. They are of a quite different nature from the initial de-animation; they admit of variation, and they appear to be in response to relatively recent requirements.

By contrast, de-animation by bleeding goes back a long way. 'You shall not eat anything that dies of itself', says the Book of Deuteronomy (14:14). Nor do we, in fact, eat either animals that died a natural or accidental death or animals killed just anyhow; we only eat livestock that has been bled by human hand. On this particular point, the regulations governing slaughtering today confirm a long tradition and meet the Mosaic requirements exactly in that bleeding is the indispensable condition for animal flesh to be prepared for butchering. The obligation is absolute, allowing of no exception. The occasional dispensation may concern the place where bleeding is carried out but never the fact of its being done.

It is usually justified on grounds of hygiene and for technical reasons: full and rapid bleeding is essential if meat is to keep well. However, it is difficult to ignore the cultural dimension completely. The need for bleeding (unlike the need for stunning) is never discussed and never has been. It seems to everyone to be natural to bleed the animals they are going to eat. The fact that they sometimes eat or drink the blood in no way affects this need to drain it from the body first. Cooking blood is one thing; eating meat that is impregnated with blood is another. When a Frenchman orders his beefsteak rare he wants it *saignant*, not *sanguinolent*.

Bleeding is the kind of obvious custom that everyone concerned takes for granted; in fact, people find it odd that anyone should remark on it. Why are animals bled? The answer, regularly, is: 'To kill them.' And the general feeling is indeed that only bleeding ensures death. But could death not be administered otherwise? 'How, then?' Various elaborations may follow: bleeding is 'simpler' or 'surer', or 'it's the way it has always been done', or 'without bleeding, the meat doesn't keep'. This much is clear: no one can imagine a different procedure. The blood must be separated from the meat, the warm and humid from the (relatively) cool and dry. Unbled meat 'goes off'; the vital principle goes into reverse when left inside a dead body. It must be separated from that body if it is not to continue to act on it. Bleeding turns an animal into something quite different from a corpse and is consequently able to dispense with further de-animalisations.

This explains why slaughtering methods have always left the moment of bleeding intact. It is invariably done with a knife,[1] by severing the blood vessels of the neck on one side only or on both sides, sometimes with a single movement amounting to semi-decapitation. Care must be taken here not to slit the rumen or oesophagus, the contents of which would taint the wound; indeed, as we shall see, endless pains are taken to get rid of blood, yet blood is not a taint like other kinds, nor does contact with it have the same polluting effect as contact with other parts of the body that dressing will do away with.

In the region studied here, no one practises bleeding by total decapitation. Moreover, the sight of calves being decapitated in Franju's film (made in the abattoirs of La Villette and Vaugirard) aroused strong revulsion among slaughtermen. 'That is barbarous,' they would say. Here, on the other hand, decapitation and removal of feet are done immediately after bleeding. Bleeding by decapitation might therefore be regarded as saving time. Instead it is seen as blurring the distinction between bleeding and dressing and perhaps even more as being unacceptable because excessive: there is 'no need to cut off the head' to bleed an animal. Whether effected by slitting the throat or making a 'buttonhole' incision, bleeding always involves a cut in the neck region, provoking fatal anaemia.

The only major change has to do with the position of the animal. Traditionally, bleeding was done with the animal lying down, either on the ground or on a cradle; nowadays vertical bleeding is compulsory, at least in abattoirs licenced for export (EC standards).

On this point European doctrine aims above all at simplification: flaying in the horizontal position is simply equated with the old practice of flaying *on the floor*, the disadvantages of which as regards the cleanliness of the meat are obvious and beyond dispute (Aufrant *et al.*, 1974, p. 56).

[1] Bleeding by trocar will be examined later in this chapter (see pp. 84–5 and figure 28). But a trocar is primarily, like a knife, a cutting blade.

Such formal simplification is somewhat over-hasty, since the vertical position does not permit the blood to drain as completely as might be imagined. The same source goes on:

> Verticality does not in itself present any particular hygiene advantage ... While for all practical purposes blood has ceased to drain from the suspended carcass, when it is lowered onto the cradle a *substantial* flow of residual blood is observed, due to the change in the position of the limbs and to a general stretching of the musculature giving way to a compression of the body under its own weight. The fact is so evident that particularly exacting butchers will sometimes ask for the operation to be repeated several times. So if vertical bleeding is to be preferred, maintaining the carcass in that position does not, despite appearances, favour complete bleeding.

It is perhaps useful to recall that, in order to get rid of as much of the blood as possible, horizontal bleeding of large bovines used to be accompanied by a process known as *foulage* [the vintner's 'pressing', the metalworker's 'ramming' (e.g., of sand)]: 'After bleeding, a rope was attached to the bullock's left forefoot and an assistant would use this to impart a to-and-fro movement in order to activate the flow of blood' (Chaudieu 1970, p. 72). Bleeding, then, is not only killing but also as complete a separation as possible between body and blood.

Consequently, throughout the dressing process cloths were used to mop up any remaining traces of blood. Today the use of cloths is banned; instead hoses, placed conveniently within reach, are employed to wash down carcasses as often as necessary.[2] Finally, slaughtermen who have acquired the habit through long experience still use the back of the knife to squeeze out any blood that rises to the surface of the meat as they work. As if in a compulsive repetition of the initial separation, numerous actions are performed to complete the draining of the blood, actions that are not restricted to the time (or, in abattoirs equipped with slaughter lines, the space) set aside for the process. So bleeding is more than just opening the mortal wound; it is also (in fact, above all) making the flesh bloodless.

This explains why the whole slaughterhall is insulated from the 'dirty' and 'clean' sectors, neither of which is in any way bloody. Even if bleeding takes place in a separate room, its repercussions are felt throughout the slaughterhall, where progress towards the 'clean' sector may be traced on the floor in terms of the gradual disappearance of bloodstains. Correlatively, the labels 'dirty' and 'clean', emanating from a hygiene point of view, seem like a shift of emphasis, as if to avoid putting a name to the site of the greatest symbolic taint: the scene of the disjunction – and hence contact (conjunction) – between 'clean' and 'dirty'.

On the other hand, the commonest, most persistent images of the abattoir

[2] And even beyond what is necessary. The technical literature contains frequent warnings against excessive hosing-down of carcasses.

are quite correct in that it is indeed a bloody place. And the revulsion that those images inspire stems precisely from the fact that they reduce the abattoir to this central place and to the blood that is shed there.

Blood made visible

If bleeding makes flesh bloodless, its corollary is to make blood visible, and it is this that sticks in the mind – even of the person who has never seen an abattoir. Because making blood visible means making it logically ambivalent and hence psychologically disturbing.

Enclosed within the body that it secretly (because invisibly) animates, blood unequivocally denotes life, whether this is understood as the vital principle itself or as the particular form it assumes in each individual being.

However, since it is the essential vital fluid, separating it from the body (and making it visible) may, in exhibiting life, bring about death. Blood becomes redly evident at moments when, however fleetingly, life and death are at stake; all visible blood is an image of present life *and* a sign of potential death. Meaning will swing between the two, depending on the occasion, but they will never be completely dissociated from each other; the ambiguity will never be entirely removed. The reason may be simply that a benign effusion is distinguished from a mortal effusion only by the quantity of blood shed. There is always the fear that it may pour forth irrepressibly.

However, there is another difference that separates two kinds of bloodshed: the one distinguishing blood that a person *sees* flowing from blood that a person *causes* to flow (Héritier [1979b] 1984–5, pp. 7–21). The latter, whatever form it may take, presupposes an assault on the integrity of the body in the sense that violence is committed against it, with or without consent.

In an abattoir, the slaughter of animals cannot be seen as proceeding by consent. The very scale on which such slaughter is conducted gives it a violent character, for even in the absence of any brutality the animals are the undifferentiated objects of a utilitarian transformation. There is no question, as in Greek sacrifice (Détienne/Vernant 1979), of requiring an appearance of consent from each animal, thus giving it a sort of social existence and making its blood the sign of a contract. In industrial slaughtering, the animals are as if dead already, their individual lives abolished by their number, with the result that, in the absence of actual violence, simply treating them like objects ('without anger and without hatred, like a butcher', to quote Baudelaire again) itself looks like violence, less visible but all the more appalling for that. This is probably also why the blood shed in abattoirs bears a heavier connotation of death than, for example, the blood of the pig or sheep slaughtered for domestic consumption. Between 'killing the pig' and bleeding pigs in series on a slaughter line there is a great gulf fixed, and it is called quantity. The two operations are definitely not of the same nature.

Visible, fatal, violent, the blood spilled in abattoirs inspires fear among those who spill it. The symbolism of bloodshed caused by wounding has repercussions even here, because if the fact of causing bloodshed is more fundamental than the blood itself, all men who are in the habit of shedding blood belong in one and the same category, and there is a blurring of the difference between animal and human blood.

Back in the days when slaughtering was done in the middle of towns, the butchers who worked and lived on terms of familiarity with blood were already credited with possessing a violent and brutal character. Whatever their means and whatever their skill, 'master butchers live by slitting the throats of animals and will always, even if it is only metaphorically, have blood under their fingernails' (Gascar 1973, p. 66). Moving abattoirs out of towns undoubtedly contributed towards relieving butchers of images of bloody brutality, but only the more effectively to transfer those images to the men who henceforth did nothing but slaughtering. Blood not only spattered their clothing; it appeared to impart a moral stain as well, either in terms of the sight of blood making men bloodthirsty or in terms of their sanguinary occupation attracting already 'sanguine' temperaments. It was the 'double corruption' that annoyed the author of the eighteenth-century *Tableau de Paris*, Louis-Sébastien Mercier (quoted in Farge 1979b, p. XX). And it was what, a century later, worried Baillet when, among other disadvantages, he blamed the 'concentration of abattoirs in one place' (he was talking about the Parisian quarter of La Villette) for

> *contributing towards demoralisation* by virtue of the nature and number of the assorted and scarcely moral elements attracted there by such a multiplicity of jobs, whereas in a smaller establishment, the influence of public opinion making itself felt more effectively, emulation operates in the direction of good rather than in that of evil (Baillet 1880, p. 537).

The figure of the slaughterman [*tueur*], poorly euphemised as 'abattoir lad' [*garçon d'abattoir*] right up until the middle of this century, was even more disturbing than that of the butcher, for no longer was it rehabilitated either by skill or by bourgeois status.

5 'I DON'T LIKE BLEEDING CALVES'

'Me, I've done pressure points, all that, that's fine, I don't get the wind up. But I'll tell you one thing, I don't like bleeding calves. It's something I just can't do. Makes me nervous, I can't do it. Working on a dead animal, all right, I couldn't care less. But bleeding calves, that I can't do. I did maybe ten after I started at ... No messing with me after that, I'm telling you! I don't like it, uh-huh. Anyway, I told the boss: you keep me on this, I'm off! Oh yes, oh yes, I told him, I did ... Also the bloke [who bleeds the calves] gets kicked in the teeth quite a bit, because calves, you know ... No, I don't like that. I don't like it!'

Such images of bloodthirsty brutality are not absent from abattoirs themselves. However, they are attributed to the past: 'In the old days, oh no, it wasn't the same'; in the old days 'you'd have found the dregs of society, you couldn't have stood it, there were some good blokes, but there were some madmen too'. Various anecdotes followed. 'The old days' were before the reorganisation of abattoirs in the 1960s. That reorganisation is generally felt to have called a halt (or provided the means of calling a halt) to various disorders by banning alcoholic drinks and dangerous amusements, controlling hygiene and humane conditions of slaughter, modernising plant, and adopting the principle of the single commercial operator. Hours and conditions of work have changed a great deal. Time spent in the abattoir is now a working day that invariably begins very early (between 4 and 6 a.m.) but does not continue indefinitely on the grounds that slaughtering may be required later in the day: 'You started at 3 in the morning and carried on till 11 at night. That's how it used to be.' 'Sometimes you were there till midnight, "they" would bring you animals to slaughter at any time of the day or night, and you had to do it, otherwise "they" would get it done somewhere else.' 'They' were the butchers and/or wholesalers who had their slaughtering done by craftsman-slaughterers. Competition, conflicts between individuals and with authorities, and long periods of hanging about with nothing to do must all have contributed to a certain atmosphere of tension. But it is hard to be sure how much is true and how much exaggeration born of a desire to demonstrate what progress has been made.

On the other hand, it seems certain that small abattoirs were less exposed to such disorders. Each butcher came to slaughter his livestock there, or to have it slaughtered by one or two assistants who then completed their day's work at the shop. Recalling the old days in small abattoirs tends, in fact, to turn into something of a lament for lost skills; the days were long and working conditions tough, but 'people knew what they were doing'. In this respect too, industrial slaughtering seems to have introduced important differences in habits and customs.

Nowadays, these images of bloodthirsty cruelty attaching to abattoirs and slaughtermen tend to be rejected. They are put down to a misunderstanding of slaughtering and a lack of coherence in people's demands: 'They want to eat meat, but it's wrong to kill animals!' As for slaughtering, 'it's supervised, we don't just do as we like'. The fact remains that 'people think we're savages', and here the rebuttals will sometimes turn vehement, leading in the end to protestations along the lines of 'there's blood and blood'. In other words, familiarity with the blood of animals does not blunt a person's sensibilities where human blood is concerned. On the contrary, nearly everyone claimed to be particularly sensitive to the sight of human blood. Often proffered without the slightest reticence, this admission is pregnant with significance. Professing a quite different reaction to human blood indicates the distinction between the blood of animals and the blood of humans and thus between 'slaughterer' and 'savage'; it is a question of combating the prejudicial assumption of a general insensitivity regarding all blood. However, this also means that the abattoir imposes the blood = death equation, with the result that any shedding of blood becomes a threat of death and the threshold of tolerance of the sight of human blood is lowered – and lowered the more sharply for the fact that such heightened sensitivity at the same time constitutes a defence mechanism. It is precisely because the blood of animals is visible everywhere that human blood must remain invisible: 'I can't stand it, I look the other way.' A male sensitivity that anywhere else would probably be seen as unmanly here simply makes a man human, makes him normal. It seeks to refute the images of cruelty derived from the analogy between all blood and human blood.

As for the sight of animal blood, 'you get used to it'. That means, of course, first facing up to its omnipresence in the slaughterhall, and this is the very first endurance test for new recruits. Mention was made of certain men whom the sight of 'all that blood' immediately put off. Occasionally a person will admit to having needed 'some time' to get used to it. But the crucial test, as we shall see, is olfactory. Sight is able to unfocus itself at will, turn aside, concentrate on the particular job in hand. 'Getting used to it' means in fact ceasing to see, ceasing to represent to oneself what one sees: 'you pay no attention to it'. Nevertheless, increasing efforts are made to get rid of the blood, to make it, so far as possible, truly invisible.

Waste or food?

The parts of the body that are successively removed to obtain a carcass may be divided into three categories:

edible by-products, i.e., offal, both red and white (see below, ch. 5, n. 1), which is processed immediately after slaughtering in tripe-dressing rooms and gut rooms;

non-edible by-products such as hides but also sometimes horns, hoofs, teeth, etc.;

and lastly waste, a less clear-cut category because all the material that is sent for rendering could equally go into the previous category: it will be used after conversion. Organic waste (dung), which used to be drained off through the sewers, is also now starting to be converted (into compost), with the result that soon nothing will be thrown away at all. This may be seen as a particular case of a general policy of waste conversion, inaugurating a 'cycle of refuse that is swift, regular, and odourless' (Corbin 1984, p. 132). Still, the category 'waste' needs to be retained because it is confirmed in everyday language and practice. In abattoirs, faecal matter and residues destined for rendering are definitely seen as waste.

What about blood?

Depending on the circumstances, blood may come into any of the above categories. It may be collected for purposes of consumption (this applies particularly to pig's blood). It may also be recovered for industrial purposes unconnected with food. Finally, it may be washed down the sewers as waste.

In the abattoirs studied here, the latter case is by far the most common. The concrete floor of the slaughterhall contains drain openings towards which all the liquid effluent, most of which is blood, is sluiced by powerful water sprays.

Water is in fact the constant antidote to blood in this place – and apparently, in varying degrees, always has been. Slaughterhouses, like other polluting establishments, were whenever possible sited near rivers or streams, into which they emptied all their waste. When abattoirs moved out of towns, they stayed near running water. Still today, abattoirs in south-west France that have not been moved recently are sited near rivers and streams. Even if preliminary purification now ensures that it no longer bears any visible traces, a watercourse is nearly always a good pointer towards an abattoir.

Because while water can always dilute blood, it is even better if it can carry it away. For this kind of cleaning, as for others, running water is obviously the best; the biggest single advance in abattoir cleaning was the installation of water sprays. Running water within easy reach will flush down the drain blood that stagnant water could only dilute:

> In the tiny courtyards of the butchers' shops . . . blood ran in the open, gushing down the street, covering the pavement with a brownish glaze, decomposing in the cracks . . . All stagnant water constitutes a threat. It is movement that purifies. A current will wash away, break down, and dissolve the organic debris that lodges in the interstices of aquatic particles. (Corbin 1982, pp. 35–6)

So whether it dilutes or carries away, water is blood's liquid antithesis. Colourless and clear, it alone is capable of dealing with that red, viscous fluid as with all bodily secretions. Like the body, blood must be washed; it must also be washed away, soaked out [the French word *essanger* (*sang* = blood) denotes the soaking of soiled linen prior to boiling]. There are some remarkable parallels between practices directed at physical cleanliness and practices directed at getting rid of blood. We know that for a long time bodily hygiene consisted in wiping the body and mopping up secretions while scrupulously avoiding direct contact with water, even using the body's own secretions to protect it (Loux/Richard 1978; Corbin 1982; Perrot 1984; Vigarello 1985; Goubert 1986). Clean, white linen, on the other hand, was an eminent sign of cleanliness; people washed their linen rather than their bodies (Verdier 1979). Similarly, blood on carcasses was, as we have seen, mopped up with cloths, and a good butcher made it a point of honour that the cloths should be perfectly white and frequently replaced. For a long time, hosing carcasses down with water met with hostility from the professionals. Water, then, was accepted as the supreme cleansing agent, but it must never come into contact with the body, so great was people's respect for its power as a solvent. On the contrary, our learning to wash with water involved a change in our representation not only of the body but also of the properties of water. Its clarity and revivifying power were the qualities that now came to be appreciated. Running water, forever renewed, bright and clear, became the image and the instrument of the new cleanliness. It was seen as capable of washing the body clean of its secretions without threatening its integrity. Little by little, showering took the place of wiping – for carcasses, too. Above all, though, easily available running water propelled before it and sent swirling down the sewers the blood that had previously hung around in a diluted state in gutters. An underground current added invisibility to the movement.

6 'CHILLING HAS NUMBED YOUR PROFESSIONAL CONSCIENCE'

'In abattoirs, is there not something that's amazed you? The slitting open of animals, and the hosing-down. It's appalling, that, absolutely appalling! Slitting open with electric tools is really bad. Because the sawblade spins too fast, the meat gets cooked beneath the bones. They've already found in certain cases that ... oh yes, everything has to go too fast, because its always: profit, profit, profit! But profit ought to be reined in, really, when things start getting catastrophic! And then there's the hosing-down afterwards. It's a fact, plenty of vets who were once all for hosing-down are starting to have second thoughts. All right, you hose down, you wash the animal. But think of the psychology of the thing. When the workman knows that if he makes mistakes, if he gets the meat dirty, it'll be washed afterwards, he stops taking care over his work. He doesn't take care any more! He says, oh well, it's going to be hosed down, that'll sort that out. It doesn't sort anything out! The microbes are there, proliferating. You'd think, the poor look of it at least ...'

'Meat that's been hosed down keeps less well, I've heard.'

'And it keeps less well! Oh, they thought, because it was put to chill right away, then frozen ... But it doesn't work like that! They're starting to realise that chilling is all very well but it has its limits, see? There are limits to what you can use it for. Now that's something very important, you know? I actually wonder whether hosing-down won't eventually be scrapped. Plus it leads to workmen being careless in their work ... There's the whole neck, including the bloody part, which is washed but also has to be cleaned. You throw away a kilo, a kilo and a half before you can sell the carcass.'

'Why the neck?'

'... Because people don't take care to clean it all afterwards [i.e. after bleeding]. *They hose it down and that's it. Before in abattoirs, when someone coffered an animal, you know what that is, when an animal's coffered* [i.e. imperfectly bled; see p. 34]? *Right. Well, when someone coffered an animal, the boss or the foreman didn't half give him hell! Because you had this problem ... There was such a thing as a professional conscience, see, which doesn't exist any more, chilling sort of put it to sleep. Chilling has numbed your professional conscience ... I had a lot of time for the old sort of abattoir worker, I did, there was a real craftsman. Oh, I don't despise them* [present-day abattoir workers], *but they don't interest me, except for the odd one or two!'*

Having become the supreme purifier, by the same token water became the implicit criterion of the dirtiest kind of refuse. Consequently, 'true' waste was now that which resisted water and had to be got rid of in other ways, namely the solid waste destined for the renderer. Everywhere such waste is described as the most repulsive residue of slaughtering. Unlike blood, solid waste is quite unequivocal: it represents the biological haunted by putrefaction, and it takes more than a squirt of water to get rid of it. The ubiquity of water, in making the ubiquity of blood less appalling, has shifted the heaviest pollution on to solid waste.

But blood is not always rejected; it is often collected for use as food or, less frequently, for other purposes.

Pig's blood is always used by *charcutiers* so has to be extracted very carefully and hygienically. In becoming food, blood is subject to the same precautions as any other product destined for human consumption. In the event, it also has to be prevented from clotting and defibrinated (when its coagulable lymph is removed). So pigs are bled above a trough fitted with a mechanical stirring device.

Blood collected in this way is sometimes also used as a dye in various manufacturing processes. In general, though, its colour is regarded as an obstacle to its use in food, except of course in the traditional *boudin* or blood pudding (the colour of which may vary considerably, depending on how it is prepared and cooked and the thickness of the casing used). One abattoir manager in the region studied has developed a pet food made mainly of blood, but it has yet to be marketed. Various authors have been concerned to promote blood as a foodstuff. For instance, under the title 'Blood is food' readers of the cookery journal *Petits propos culinaires* were once introduced (Siesby 1980, pp. 41–9) to the excellent nutritional properties of blood and the advantages to be had from making methodical use of them. However, an official study in France (CEMAGREF 1980, No. 6, p. 28) was forced to conclude that 'the red colouring of blood is a handicap as regards its use as human food' – unless, of course, an easy way were found of separating the red haema from the colourless globin ...

In all these culinary uses, blood is eaten after having been solidified by cooking and mixed with various ingredients. In its therapeutic uses, on the other hand, blood is consumed pure, raw, in liquid form, and fresh (i.e., still warm). The field study furnished no proof that such customs still survive, but quite a number of statements corroborated one another in suggesting that they were practised until quite recently (perhaps less than ten years ago). People who drank blood were obeying an ancient belief in its restorative properties when drunk while still warm; replete with the life of the body it had just vacated, it was thought to be capable of enlivening the drinker. As for any pleasure they may have taken in the practice, opinions differ widely.

Some will describe a respectable octogenarian, say, who used to come two of three times a week to warm the evening of his life with a large glass of calf's blood; others will recall more reluctant drinkers, so reluctant sometimes that the man who was bleeding the bullock had to 'go first'. However, familiarity with blood appears to breed no desire to drink it, even for real or imagined

7 INDUSTRIAL USES OF BLOOD

Twenty-five or thirty years ago, blood as well as guts were thrown on manure heaps and taken away by farmers, who were paid a certain sum of money per year to do the job. Around 1840, the refining of cane or beet sugar started to be done using blood. However, the blood was always poorly prepared and was only ever used by refiners with a certain amount of revulsion, a number of them preferring milk or eggs. A special department had been set up in Paris to supply refiners with some of the blood produced in abattoirs; the surplus blood was drained off into pits and mixed with lime and other absorbent materials to make fertiliser. Around 1848 someone had the idea of extracting the albumin from blood for use not only in sugar refining but also for fixing dyes in the manufacture of printed fabrics. It was the period 1860 to 1875 that saw the greatest advances both in the preparation and in the use of blood, whether for industry or for agriculture, and we hasten to add that it is above all an industrialist from Ivry-sur-Seine, near Paris, one Mr. Bourgeois jr., who has been responsible for the improvements made in the processing of blood in abattoirs. Using special new techniques, Mr. Bourgeois extracts the albumin from blood and supplies it to businesses in a state of total dessication; the cruoric matter is likewise dried for use as a fertiliser. Dried albumin comes in the form of small flat fragments, yellowish in colour, semi-transparent or opaque, depending on how pure it is, and brittle. Dried cruor comes in the form of a smooth dark powder with no obvious smell and containing 12 to 13 per cent nitrogen.

Despite the advantages of removing blood from abattoirs, however, the method adopted for removing it did in certain circumstances give rise to objections, as a result of which Mr. Bourgeois had to modify his operation considerably. There follows a brief account of the modus operandi *in use today in the Bordeaux abattoir.*

The blood is collected in trays and left for several hours; the serum separates and is recovered separately, whilst the clot, divided by means of a mechanical mill, is processed in situ *with a liquid coagulant, the formula of which is known only to the inventor. After this blending, the mass assumes a brownish appearance and a smooth consistency and gives off a faintly acid odour. Left to drain and subsequently to dry, it forms a brown powder that is naturally very rich in nitrogenous matter and capable of being used as a very powerful fertiliser. The process involved offers great advantages, among which attention should be drawn above all to the possibility of dealing* in situ *and at no risk to public hygiene with the large quantity of blood collected in an abattoir daily. It further allows the blood to be transformed immediately into a magma that can then be transported in open carts without risk (as is the case when transporting liquid blood) of spilling blood on the highway travelled by the vehicles used for such transport.*

In our view, then, every encouragement should be given to this important industry of utilising the blood from abattoirs, because not only does it supply products destined to be of enormous service in the arts, commerce, and agriculture; it also permits the utilisation of a large proportion of a naturally nitrogenous substance, the decomposition of which would have disastrous consequences as regards public hygiene. (Adapted from Baillet 1880, pp. 545–6)

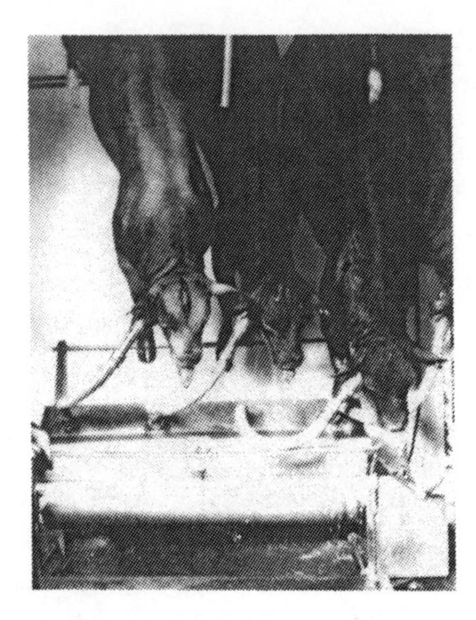

28 Bleeding by trocar

The trocar is held in the bleeding incision by means of a hook; the tank is for collecting the blood. Note the horizontal water pipe for spraying carcasses to remove any impurities that might taint the blood.

therapeutic purposes, most slaughtermen evincing a degree of scepticism. It is worth noting, at least, that pig's blood appears never to have been drunk in this way, any more than the blood of sheep or goats ('too thick', it is said); the blood that vivifies is the blood of young or adult bovines. Finally, a further therapeutic use not involving ingestion is described by one author who was prescribed baths of fresh blood to revive a leg weakened after a fracture (Genevoix 1969, pp. 9–14). Whatever the method, the principle behind it is that blood is invigorating, being life itself. Hence the need to go to the abattoir, the place where blood is to be found in its warm effusion. The ambiguity of spilled blood, indeed!

Lastly, blood may be collected for incorporation in a wide variety of industrial products ranging from cosmetics to concrete (Bouchet 1980) with numerous pharmaceutical products in between. Abattoir operators are keen to increase such reprocessing options for reasons both economic and ecological, but they are still relatively few in number. Two abattoirs in Gers recover calves' blood for the pharmaceutical industry. Obviously, such purposes require bleeding to be done in accordance with strict standards of cleanliness, and for this suitable equipment is required.

It is done, in fact, with the aid of a trocar. This involves 'piercing a large-diameter blood vessel with a special draining knife, the trocar, which is pushed in up to the hilt and held in that position throughout the bleeding

29 Recovery of blood

From the recovery tank the blood is transferred to a cooling tank fitted with a mechanical stirring device

process' (CEMAGREF 1980, No. 6, p. 21). Blood 'gathered' in this way runs down a pipe called a cannula into a trough, where it is stirred mechanically; it is then sucked up through pipework and poured into a refrigerated vat before being put into tanks and kept in the coldstore. There, frozen solid, it is stacked in calibrated blocks. Blood, yes, but clean, aseptic. A lorry calls to collect it once or twice a month.

All that is needed to recover blood in this way, apart from suitable plant, is one extra worker to see to the freezing and above all to the upkeep of the premises, troughs, and tanks. In one case this job was done by a young woman, whose husband was in charge of bleeding by trocar. She happened to have worked in a dairy before, and after remarking that the same meticulous cleanliness was required in both cases, right down to using the same cleaning products, she concluded her comparison with the words: 'Milk and blood, it's the same thing.' What on the contrary is totally different is the image that 'people' have of the two jobs: 'when you say you work at the abattoir ...', it is brought home to you that milk does not involve animals dying, that its whiteness gives it an appearance of innocence that blood can never possess, and that the red colour of blood comes off on people who get close to it.

The ambiguity of spilled blood – as waste or commodity, medicine or food (though never excrement), depending on the circumstances – is evident here in its taxonomic lability: 'As pure as it is impure, as healthy as it is unhealthy,

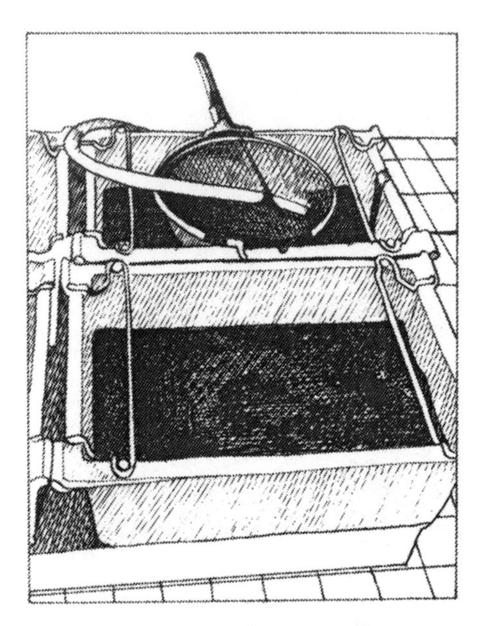

30 It is then filtered and collected in tubs

31 The tubs are stacked for storage in the freezer room

as much a sign of life as a harbinger of death and slaughter, it flows out and away without ever allowing itself to be definitely classified as being on one side or the other' (Fargo 1979b, p. XV). Far from reducing this ambiguity, abattoir practice exploits it; any category will do, so long as the blood dis-

32 A workstation for stunning and bleeding ovines

Animals are first stunned on the floor with the aid of electrodes, then hoisted on to an overhead track and bled above the grating. The V-shaped hole in the wall between stunning and bleeding allows the suspended animal to pass through as it is being hoisted up. A gate closes off the passage in the right foreground while slaughtering is taking place.

appears most effectively. Because the sight of it is not everything. Even when it has disappeared completely and the abattoir is empty with the concrete floor well hosed down after work, blood remains an invisible presence. The smell of it lingers on, diffuse, more persistent than the substance itself, evoking its presence even when the substance itself has gone.

The smell of blood

It is in the nature of every smell to emanate and to be inhaled; all 'smelling' presupposes the transitive as well as the intransitive construction [this applies to the French *sentir* as much as to the English 'smell']. It follows that a smell gives away the thing from which it rises, even if that thing is invisible, having been removed. Also it permeates whoever breathes it in – physically, like every other object in the space through which it spreads, and psychologically, too, when the physical sensation is bound up with feelings. Brillat-Savarin's famous dictum about eating habits might well be plagiarised as: 'Tell me what you *smell/smell of*, and I will tell you who you are' – the more legitimately, in fact, since smell is closely linked to taste. Rousseau (see *Émile*, book II) believed that together they formed the sense of incorporation.

The sight of the blood spilled in an abattoir is, as we have seen, the first

33 General view of a slaughter line for large bovines

On the right is the platform for flaying flanks; on the left, the chute for evacuating white offal through a hatch to the *coche*;* between them, a waste bin; above, the overhead track from which the animals are suspended.

* Yard, also known as a *voirie* ['refuse dump'], in abattoirs set aside to receive the waste matter obtained from emptying the animals' stomachs and intestines' (*Littré*, supplement [1879] to the 1878 edition). Nowadays the *coche* is a room fitted out to handle the disposal of waste.

endurance test. The smell of it is the second, and it is the crucial one. Though it is registered before sight, and its assault on the senses is as violent, it makes its effect felt over time. When a man refuses from the first moment to work in an abattoir, his defection is never attributed to smell alone but rather to the sight of blood; the most that will be suggested is that 'maybe the smell too' was more than he could bear. But if he quits the job after three or six months, it will be because he cannot get used to the smell. 'It was the smell, the chap couldn't eat any more,' I was told about one man. 'What, not eat meat any more?' 'No, he couldn't eat at all.' There are not many such cases, but they are significant, both as regards the link between smell and taste and as regards the way smell works. Unlike sight, which is a highly intellectualised sense (to the point where [in both French and English] 'to see' often means 'to understand'), olfaction seems to somatise its effects more: 'Smell disturbs the psychism more profoundly than hearing or sight; it appears to reach down to the roots of life', notes Corbin after reviewing various theories (Corbin 1982, pp. V–VI). Similarly, Lévi-Strauss observes that the sense of smell is 'of all the

34 A slaughter line for ovines

The door on the left leads to the stunning room. The carcasses, suspended after bleeding, are lowered on to cradles that revolve and rock on their supports. When not in use, the cradles come to rest in the lowest position. At the end of the line, the carcasses are re-suspended and moved on towards the flaying machine (out of picture; figure 44 shows it in use).

senses the one most deeply rooted in organic life' (Lévi-Strauss 1971, p. 587). If knowing [*savoir*] does bear some relation to savour [*saveur*, from the same Latin root *sapere*], as Serres contends (Serres 1985), it is an obscurely inward kind of knowing, a confused reminiscence. Provençal French (the *langue d'oc*) commonly uses *savoir à* in the sense of 'to taste of, smell like, or look like (something)', that is to say to have some trace, whether gustatory or olfactory, that instinctively recalls something familiar. In other words, the sense of taste, associated with the sense of smell, is 'an emotional reaction to the relevant stimulus' (Chive, 1979, p. 108).

Still, most of the time people do 'get used to it' (i.e., to the smell as well as to the sight) and, come the mid-morning break, everyone tucks in with a hearty appetite. Some remember a time when there was no canteen and they had to eat their snack in the actual slaughterhall, at least in winter. Others will remark that the smell of carcasses, or even of animals, 'doesn't give you silicosis' or that 'it's not unhealthy – we eat meat, don't we?' Without being quite as explicit, such comments recall the opinion expressed by the butchers who, according to one eighteenth-century source, 'ascribe the good health that most of them enjoy to inhaling the smells of the blood, fat, and entrails of the animals they slaughter' (Corbin, 1982, p. 248). People at least draw a distinction between the inconvenient and the insalubrious. However, a degree of inconvenience remains unavoidable, and everyone will refer to the waste destined for the renderer as nauseating, never going near it unless they have to. Olfactory sensibility combines with visual sensibility, explaining why part of the power of water and cold stems from the fact that they 'improve the air' (Vigarello 1985, p. 164) and avert or disperse smells. The worst kind of waste is both visible and foul smelling.

Habituation, then, can raise a person's threshold of tolerance, but only so far. It is the same with smell as with sight: no one can be impervious to everything. Unlike visual habituation, however, the olfactory inhibition is not acquired once and for all. A person returning from holiday needs to become re-habituated; he has to reconquer the olfactory assault that itself returns with renewed vigour for several days following the period when it was in abeyance. It is then, too, that a person becomes aware that smell operates by permeation, by contaminating the body in such a way that the smell one inhales almost without noticing it any more becomes the smell that one exhales [in the sense of gives off], a stubborn trace that, by clinging to the skin, gives one away. Just as the Minot peasants change their clothes to get rid of the 'smell of the cowshed' (Pingaud 1978, p. 246), slaughterers shower and change before leaving the abattoir. Despite this, their nearest and dearest can still detect 'the smell', even if, being used to it themselves, they no longer say anything. The interruption represented by holidays, in decontaminating a person from the smell, causes him to rediscover its presence and its effects, lending its weight of truth to the outward admission: 'when I come back I realise my wife is right' (in saying, like many others, that her husband 'smells of the abattoir'). The transitive and intransitive uses of 'to smell' vary in inverse proportion to one another: a person smells (perceives the smell) less, the more he smells (gives off the smell) himself, and conversely. However, working in an abattoir, he can never not smell, in one way or another.

'The smell' (without closer definition) or 'the abattoir smell' is, one is told, 'the smell of blood'. The uninitiated nose is inclined to think otherwise, believing it is registering a composite odour, acrid and powerful, like a cowshed, butcher's shop, and tripe shop rolled into one.

Talking about the smell that permeates them, slaughterers draw a clear distinction between the smell of pigs and all the other smells: 'When a man does pigs, you know about it, he has the smell.' However, it is difficult to state that the smell is particularly related to the animals. If the pig line does smell different, it is partly because pigs are not flayed. The steam from the scalding plant is mingled with the smells of gas and burning hair, of blowlamps or flamethrowers; the humid atmosphere gives the impression of being more heavily impregnated. Moreover, pig blood is usually recovered for sale to the *charcuterie* trade, and it may be that its visible presence makes people more aware of its smell.

However, even if there is agreement about its composite nature, the 'abattoir smell' is defined by the 'smell of blood', or at least people will claim to distinguish the smell of blood clearly from all the others. The ultimate proof that the smell of blood is quite distinct and perceptible, that it is 'not a fancy', is found in the sensitivity of animals in this regard: 'the animals smell it'.

Generally speaking, animals are credited with much better noses than humans, and studies of animal behaviour (CEMAGREF 1982b) confirm that the sense of smell is on the whole more highly developed in livestock than in humans. However, the claim that animals register the smell of blood is more than a simple statement of fact; it is accompanied by the notion that, smelling blood (their own blood), animals sense what is in store for them. The sense of smell is the sense of premonition, obscure yet certain, and as such is said to account for the behaviour of restive animals.

This view, though widespread, is by no means uniformly shared. Some people refuse to credit animals with any real understanding while nevertheless according them the privilege of more acute senses, particularly as regards smell, though only in differential terms in that animals are thought to notice (and be disturbed by) anything unusual, even where it does not represent a danger. Thus transportation, handling, unfamiliar places, and strange stablemates give rise to stress, they say, without such perceptions being accompanied by any kind of premonition. Often, too, people will confine themselves to pointing out that animals facing slaughter are on the whole more docile and more manageable than they would be if they understood anything of what was going on, also that they can be deceived by gentleness, which would not be the case if the notorious smell of blood had any clear, precise significance.

As witness this account:

> No more than the sheep, no more than the lambs, and no more than the bullocks did the calves take fright at the smell of blood rising from the great vats in the shed where swollen paunches floated like clothes in the washtub. No animal ever balked at that abstract, purely mythical line separating the world of blood from the rest of the place, from the sky, from the three young elms. The only place that caused them a moment's alarm was the dead end down which pools of water gleamed and metal hooks reflected rays of light, that too brightly lit retreat where the 'dressed' lamb swung ceaselessly, pinkly, with, around its neck, a broad paper ruff arranged just beneath the missing head, now lying in a corner, a bloody bucranium (Gascar, 1953, pp. 46–70).

This is a telling description. The astonishing thing is that, smelling and seeing everything, the animals remain docile, and a vague sense of guilt, a feeling of disloyalty on man's part, arises from this very trust that animals evince in a place where everything *ought to* alert them. In killing them in spite of all this, one is taking advantage of their stubborn ignorance.

By contrasting the objectively disturbing clues with the total absence of fear on the animal's part, literary analysis reveals a negative of the mechanism of projection that unconsciously operates in reality: since, like humans, they are endowed with senses (superior senses, so far as smell is concerned), animals have attributed to them perhaps not precisely the kind of clear understanding that men possess but at least an intuition, a vague presentiment. It seems inconceivable that sensory perception should not induce signification. The fact that animals *sentent* ['perceive through the senses', but also literally 'smell'] necessarily means that they *pressentent* ['experience foreboding']. And discourse embarrasses itself when it seeks to separate the two [*sentir* and *pressentir*], so closely are they linked in common parlance, for which the sense of smell is the faculty of intuition.

The spread of people's opinions regarding what the smell of blood means to animals does not coincide with the spread of their educational backgrounds and rational knowledge concerning animals. A slaughterman or, say, a vet, is as likely to be a Cartesian as a Pythagorean, as likely to be a mechanist as a vitalist. This suggests that, in the comparison of animal and human feelings with regard to spilled blood, what is at issue is a theory of man. More directly it suggests that the question of a good or bad conscience in connection with the slaughter of animals touches on the legitimisation of human actions and of the order instituted by man.

On one point at least, everyone is agreed: sight is not, for animals, a source of signification but purely a stimulus. Smell, however, does seem to be the principal sense behind an animal's awareness, its significance being grasped but not represented: osmosis between the body and the air it breathes brings about an *incorporation* of meaning such that 'smell' is indeed what French calls *science infus* ['innate knowledge']. Men and animals differ here in that sight and smell seem to vary in inverse proportion to each other. For men, olfaction may well have subtle long-term effects through the way in which it immerses them too in ambient odours. However, it is not in itself a source of meaning; it becomes fully effective in terms of meaning only when backed up by sight. Without the aid of the other senses, particularly sight, smell merely confuses. This is verified, as it were experimentally, by the purely olfactory discovery of the abattoirs of Chicago by Upton Sinclair's Lithuanian immigrants:

Along with the thickening smoke, they began to notice another circumstance, a strange, pungent odor. They were not sure that it was unpleasant, this odor; some might have called it sickening, but their taste in odors was not developed, and they were only sure that it was curious ... It was now no longer something far off and faint, that you caught in whiffs; you could literally taste it, as well as smell it ... They were divided in their opinion about it. It was an elementary odor, raw and crude; it was rich, almost rancid, sensual and strong. There were some who drank it in as if it were an intoxicant; there were others who put their handkerchiefs to their faces. The new immigrants were still tasting it, lost in wonder, when suddenly the car came to a halt, and the door was flung open, and a voice shouted out – 'stockyards' (Sinclair [1906] 1974, p. 32).

This makes it even more significant that the smell of abattoirs should be interpreted as 'the smell of blood'. The reduction of a complex affluvium to one of its components derives from something other than olfaction alone. By releasing the blood that the live body held captive, the operation of bleeding gives to blood its full ambiguity and symbolic power. Ultimately, the 'smell of blood' is the Greek *miasma*, the defilement of spilled blood; it permeates minds as much as space and things. In spilled blood the death-dealing aspect of carnivorous man becomes palpable, and complex relationships condense between men and animals. In a different register, these go on to develop fresh effects.

5

MEN AND ANIMALS

How tools form a hierarchy

When empty and not in use, a slaughterhall looks much like any other industrial workplace. The cleaners have piled the solid waste into bins. Water has washed away all trace of blood and purified the air. The ceramic tiles on the walls and the cement floor shine from their final rinse. If one did not already know, the machines and the various pieces of equipment would give little idea of the kind of work that has gone on here. To disturb the calm, it would be necessary to name each object.

The fact is, the most immediately significant tool is put away after work. The first thing a man does on leaving the hall is to unbuckle the belt that carries the knife-holster and steel (for sharpening knives) that are the true tools of the trade and that, as soon as work finishes, are cleaned and locked away in the cloakrooms. The typical abattoir tool, the one in constant use or always within reach, thus disappears at the same time as the men. All the hand tools, the choppers and saws used for cutting off horns, sawing through the rib cage, and splitting pigs and bovines, disappear likewise.

All these tools are gradually giving way to machines, which make the work less laborious. Hand saws and choppers are being replaced by electric saws and cutting pliers; sheep are sometimes flayed with pulling machines or with a machine that approximately reproduces the movements of the traditional 'punching' with the fist. The old straw torches used for singeing pigs disappeared in the immediate post-war period at the latest, to be replaced by machines for scalding, dehairing, and singeing or by simple blowlamps.

The knife itself has been replaced by the so-called 'Perco' flaying machine (a hand-held circular saw known to English slaughtermen as a 'strimmer'; see figure 21). However, it is still indispensable at several stages of the flaying process, starting with the initial slitting of the skin along a line that will give the hide as regular a shape as possible (Chaudieu 1975, pp. 82–3; see figure 36), and it is often with the aid of a knife that the flayer begins the task of separating the hide from the carcass. Subsequently, it is indispensable for the evisceration of both chest and abdominal cavities, where it is used to open the ventral wall and sever the internal attachments of the entrails. Lastly, on

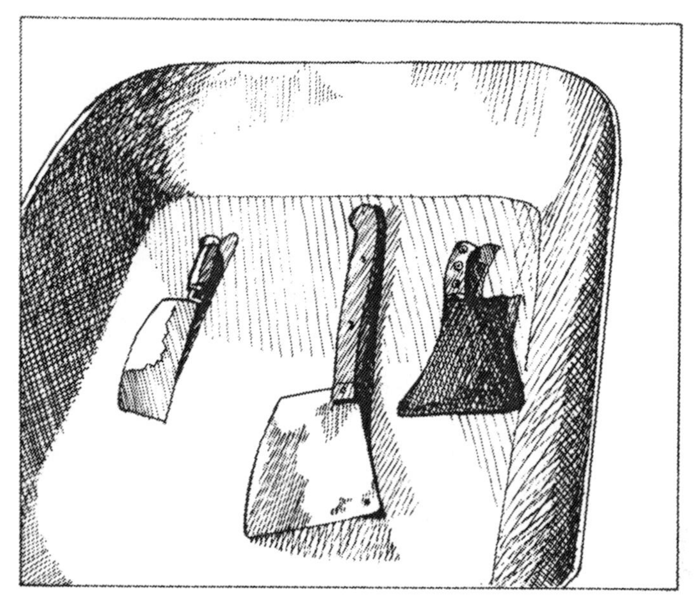

35 Hand tools

These are increasingly being replaced by electric tools for splitting carcasses.

calves and sheep the leg joints are severed with a knife, as is the head in all species, whether it is removed before or after flaying. And above all the knife is the essential tool for bleeding. For all these reasons knives are omnipresent; the knife is the tool *par excellence*, always carried, always kept razor-sharp.

The knife is in fact the yardstick and the badge of skill. Older slaughtermen, those who were apprenticed on the job from the age of twelve or fourteen, all describe the same 'training path'. First they were given the humblest jobs, cleaning the premises and equipment. Then, still cleaning, they were assigned to the 'white offal',[1] the heads and feet that had to be scalded and then lengthily scraped to rid them of all hair, using an old blunt knife or the back of a good knife. At this stage they were also given all the main gut-dressing jobs, which were repulsive and required no particular skill. Little by little they started to work on carcasses, severing feet, heads, and horns, beginning with marking out, and eventually doing evisceration, flaying

[1] 'The term *white offal* is applied to the entrails and such parts of the animal as head, feet, and stomachs that, once scalded or dehaired, have the colour of ivory.

'By *red offal* we mean such parts of the animal as cheeks, tongue, brains, lungs, heart, spleen, liver, sweetbreads, etc. They are so called, in contrast to white offal, because of their red or pink colour' (Chaudieu 1970, p. 13).

It may also be noted that only white offal requires protracted cleaning, whereas red offal is virtually taken straight from the carcass.

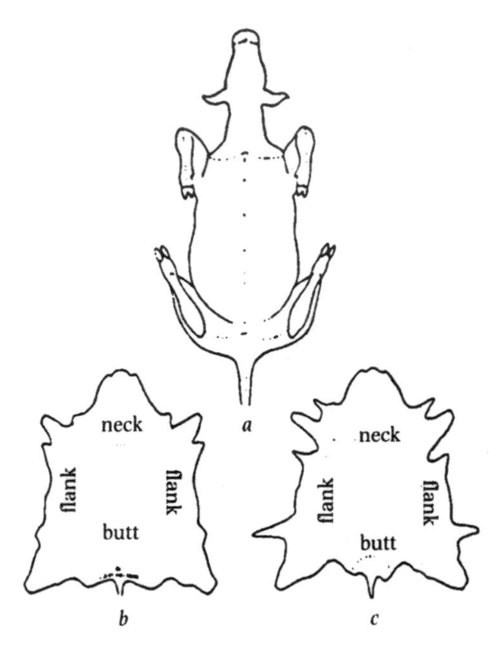

36 Removing a hide (diagrams from Chaudieu 1975, pp. 82–3)

Figure (a) shows the animal in the supine position. To cut the hide correctly, first make an opening from head to tail, cutting straight and cleanly, right in the centre, without wandering to either side.

Then make the transverse openings, following the lines indicated in the diagram; that is to say, when opening up the thighs avoid doing down into the tail, and when opening up the chest take care to follow the line indicated.

Figure (b) shows a hide cut according to the above instructions. Note that it is square in shape and the flanks leave the maximum width, allowing generous use.

Figure (c) shows a badly cut hide. Note that it has long tongues on either side as well as deep indentations, which give it an awkward shape and limit its usefulness. The flanks are irregular in shape, reducing the hide's value. Calves must be flayed in accordance with the principles set out above. Sheep pelts must also be correctly removed. Avoid holes and tears, which will reduce their value.

proper, and bleeding. The apprenticeship thus progressed from excrement ('You always started with the shit') to food, passing by way of white offal. The big day, confirming that the apprentice had learned his trade, was when the boss gave him a knife-holster and steel. There was no ceremony attached, but everyone knew that this was tantamount to an investiture. The knife is indeed the tool *par excellence*, as I say, and it is competence with the knife that makes a skilled slaughterer.

Only in flaying as such is the knife used differently in dealing with different species of animal. Three categories may be distinguished from this standpoint, involving three different methods of flaying.

37 Bleeding pigs

After being stunned with the aid of electrodes (see figure 42), pigs are suspended and hoisted to a position above a tank containing a mechanical stirrer before being bled.

Pigs are not flayed; they are cleaned instead. The hairs on the skin are removed by scalding, scraping (mechanical or manual), and singeing, and the carcass is 'finished' by scraping and hosing down. The feet are not cut off but the hooves are removed. This method of preparation is related to the work of cleaning white offal in that the essential processes are the same and use of the knife is similarly limited. Only bleeding, evisceration, and

8 'WHEN YOU'RE LEARNING'

A.: 'When you're learning, at least back when I learned the job, you learned to do everything. You learned to . . . you had to salt the hides, you had to do the offal, you had to kill the calf, hang it up, stun it, and in those days that meant by hand, we didn't use a pistol, and you did flaying and gutting, the lot . . . '

'A kid starting out, he wouldn't have to flay an animal on his first day?'

A.: 'Oh, yes he would! Oh my goodness, yes! Oh, they had to learn fast!'

B.: 'Basically, when you're starting out you always have to do the jobs the boss doesn't like doing!'

A.: 'That's right. Still, it wasn't like that with us in the old days . . . Cleaning and . . . the animals, the feet . . . What I dislike most is sheep and lamb. That's a pain. I mean to say, I get on faster, I used to work faster on bullocks, on larger animals, that is, and calves. On sheep I seem to take a long time.'

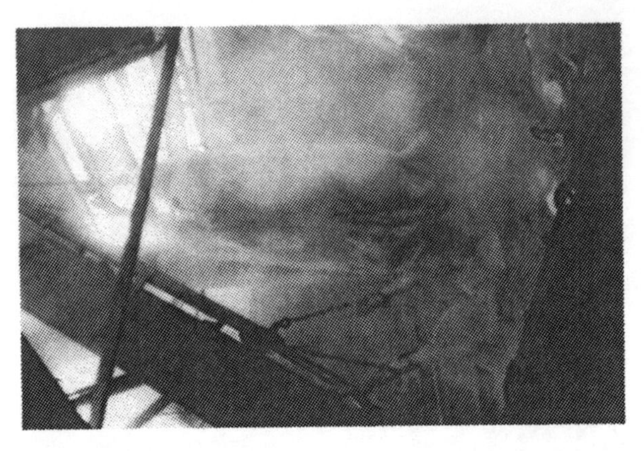

38 Scalding pigs

They are then immersed in the scalding tank, already swathed in the steam given off by water heated to around 60°C.

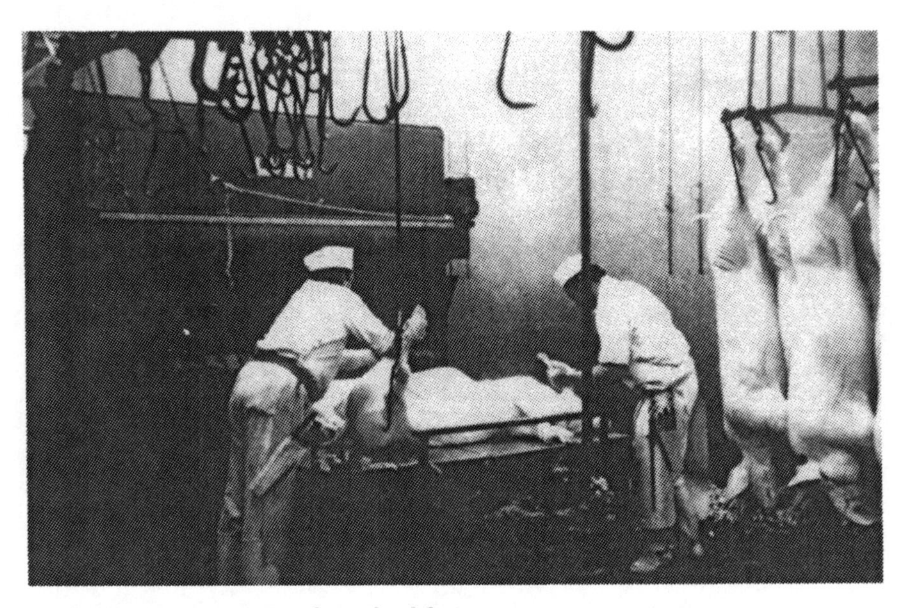

39 Pig carcasses emerging from the dehairer

Once the pig has been dehaired, the hooves and part of the head are removed and the carcass suspended from a cambrel.

40 Singeing

Following abdominal and thoracic evisceration, the animal is singed with a blowlamp. Visible in the foreground are a water spray and a four-pronged grapnel. This workstation disappears where the pig line is equipped with a dehairer with built-in singeing facility.

decapitation use the sharp edge of the knife. The final splitting in two is done with a chopper.

Ovines (sheep and lambs) are partially flayed with the knife, which is used to sever the feet, cut the first line in the pelt, and 'peel' the hind-quarters. But the bulk of flaying is done by what is called 'punching', a job that everyone agrees is extremely laborious and typifies the dressing of ovines. 'Punching' is done bare-handed, with one fist being forced between skin and flesh while the other hand holds the pelt under tension. Some abattoirs have machines to spare people the more laborious part of this process. One machine (it is actually called a 'puller') simply pulls the skin off; a more recent, more efficient machine has two articulated arms that separate the skin from the carcass by reproducing 'punching' mechanically. Whichever method is used, little use of the knife is involved.

Bovines and equines are 'peeled' completely with the knife (or with a strimmer, which performs precisely the same function).

This explains why the ultimate test of skill is being able to 'do/make an animal' and why the top 'animals' are universally considered to be the large bovines. The tool that forms a hierarchy of skills (and hence of men) at the same time forms a hierarchy of animals. Though smaller in volume than adult bovines, calves are their equivalent as regards assessing men's skills, the flaying operation being identical in both instances. At the other end of the

41 Splitting a pig carcass by hand

This is the final operation before stamping by the veterinary technicians and transfer to the cooling room. The head of each pig, completely severed, is suspended from the same cambrel as the animal.

scale, pigs are seen as being of lesser value because their preparation does not require the same total mastery of the knife. The only task regarded as difficult in the dressing of pigs is splitting the carcass in two with a chopper, which calls for immense sureness of execution. For the rest, people will say that on the pig line it is above all meticulous care that is required, whereas the 'punching' of sheep calls for strength and the flaying of bovines for skill (particularly if one is to avoid puncturing the hides).

9 'WORKING AS IF IT HAD BEEN FOR THEMSELVES'

'They say women are more careful [in the tripe-dressing room]. Is that true, do you think?'

'Absolutely, yes. Some men are meticulous too though, right? They aren't there any more, when I worked there they were taking early retirement, even reaching retirement age, some of them. No, they were ... fanatics in the tripe-dressing room, fanatics, you know?'

'What do you mean, "fanatics"? Fanatical in what sense?'

'About cleanliness. Seeing that the tripe was well done, that it was properly prepared. The pleasure of working as if it had been for themselves. For sale! Some people really adore that stuff.'

42 The sheep line: stunning and suspension

The man on the left is holding the electrical appliance with which he has just stunned the animal that can be seen in the background, being hoisted up on the rail towards the bleeding station. The man on the right is about to take another hook from the rail on the left with which to suspend the next sheep. Both men are wearing 'whites', the regulation work clothing consisting of rubber boots, cotton jacket and trousers, plastic apron, and disposable cap.

Numerous references have been made to the peculiar nature of pig slaughtering. As regards these parallel hierarchies among men and animals, in terms of the knife as major tool we find pigs placed at the bottom of the scale for the reason that they are not flayed. Now it so happens that it is on the pig line that we find the few women who work in the slaughterhall. The fact that in a hierarchy of typically male skills women are found on the bottom rung will surprise no one. Nevertheless, it is worth taking another look at this, since the matter is probably more complex than it seems.

Women and knives

The general opinion is that slaughtering is not a job for a woman. The argument put forward, of course, is women's physical frailty. However, not all slaughtering jobs call for enormous physical strength, nor are all women necessarily puny. People agreed that this was so. And they promptly cited the rare cases (two in all[2]) of women who worked as slaughterers 'like men'; they would even (the crowning humiliation) tell you about the one woman

[2] I met only one of them. The information I received about the other was insufficiently detailed to enable me to trace her.

43 The sheep line: opening-up and flaying of hindquarters

who apparently carried off a first prize in a regional flaying competition. Yet such exceptions do nothing to alter the original verdict that this is no job for women.

Nevertheless, women are still to be found in abattoirs. They work 'in the offices', of course, and in jobs connected with hygiene control; but they also work in tripe-dressing rooms, even if they no longer constitute the majority there, as they did until very recently; and lastly (less frequently) they may be found on the pig line, where they singe and 'finish' the carcasses. And that

10 'THAT, SIR, IS HOW YOU SPLIT A CALF'

'When I was young, I had a woman boss. One time this ... this lad turned up, because the foreman, I remember now, had left to set up on his own, and she thought I was a bit young to be put in charge of the stall in Tarbes market. They had a stall there. Well, I was young, I was only ... twenty, I think. Through an advertisement, they'd got in touch with a foreman in Paris. This foreman came down from Paris. He'd been to college, but you know those college types ... He couldn't split a calf. So my boss, who was fifty-three at the time, she said to him: "Here, watch this!" And she took the chopper and split the calf, one, two, three. "That, sir, is how you split a calf!"'

'Had she done it before?'

'Oh yes, she'd done it before. "That, sir, is how you split a calf!" The bloke, he was thirty-five, he didn't say a word. In any case he fell ill a fortnight later, I think it was. He just never came back' [laughter].

44 The sheep line: a flaying machine

A clamp on the end of a hinged arm holds the pelt under tension while two endless screws, first introduced together halfway up the carcass, gradually move apart, separating skin from flesh. When the first flank has been flayed, the same operation is repeated on the second.

surprises no one, because 'it's not the same'; doing such jobs, 'they're more careful' than men (who nevertheless form the majority here too). So where exactly is the dividing line between what is suitable for women and what is not?

That their presence in the tripe-dressing room and at certain workstations on the pig line seems normal provides the first clue. We have seen how the fact that pigs are not flayed makes their preparation similar to the work of processing offal in the tripe-dressing room. In both cases, what is involved is scalding, dehairing, scraping – in a word, cleaning. The work is like a blend of washing and cooking, operations that are often associated because any kind of culinary preparation includes a phase in which the ingredients are cleaned and because washing can constitute 'a complete cuisine' (Verdier 1979, p. 111). In both cases the principal aids are fire and water; the person works in the steamy humidity of scalding tanks (or soaking tubs) and in the heat of blowlamps or flamethrowers (or stoves). Such tasks have traditionally devolved upon women, and any similar task appears to fall 'naturally' into their province. This would account at the same time for the relative scorn, of which there are various shades of expression, reserved for men who only work (and only know how to work) on the pig line.

We also find, however, that in a hierarchy of jobs based on the use of the

45 The lamb line: working on a conveyor belt

Visible in the background is the carousel for draining-out after bleeding. A man unhooks the lambs from this and places them on the conveyor belt, where five men perform the initial operations of flaying: removal of fore and hind feet, opening-up of front and rear, and flaying of hindquarters. The animals are then suspended from two carousels for the remainder of the dressing process.

knife, women are missing from the top two rungs, namely bovines and sheep. Now the knife (like all the traditional slaughterhall tools, incidentally) is an ambiguous instrument:

> The same knife, used in the same percussive mode, becomes a tool or a weapon, depending on the nature of the object treated. Cutting wood makes it a tool, cutting bread makes it a table implement, unless we are talking about a baker's knife, in which case it becomes a tool. Slitting a sheep's throat likewise makes it a tool, whereas the same treatment meted out to a man makes it a weapon (Leroi-Gourhan [1943] 1971, p. 112).

Besides 'the nature of the object treated', in this context we certainly need to take equal account of the effect obtained. In skinning and evisceration, the knife is unquestionably regarded as a tool. But it can only be used as a tool in this way because it has first, at the bleeding stage, served to kill – and while killing animals ought to make it a tool, we have seen how much ambiguity there is in spilled blood. Moreover, the ambiguous status of the knife actually impinges upon awareness. It is clearly alluded to, for instance, in certain gestures that are no less significant for being only mock-serious. When a hand flies to a knife-holster, say, or a knife is raised in the air and pointed at someone, the threat is never in earnest but will effectively get rid of, say, a

46 The lamb line: 'punching'

Unlike sheep, lambs do not have their pelts slit along the stomach but are flayed 'in the round'. A puncher first flays the animal as far as the last ribs approximately; flaying is sometimes completed with the aid of a machine.

practical joker. 'A bit of fun' it may be, but it would appear that there is an awareness here, however vague, that a knife may also be a weapon.

It would seem, too, that it is this death-dealing weapon that women are kept away from, since even the women who 'work like men' do not perform bleeding.[3] Here is one of them:

No, I didn't do the killing! I didn't want to do bleeding or killing. No, sorry, I tell a lie. Calves were stunned with the pistol – I did that. But I didn't bleed. Because I'd told my husband, 'I don't want to do bleeding.' [Why was that?] *Because. I just didn't. Because that was killing the animal, and I didn't want to do that.* [And stunning with the pistol?] *Yes, stunning I did, that didn't bother me.*

Yet 'the killing has to be done, it's a job', she said a moment later. Obviously, though, it is not a job for a woman. The result is that women have the use of the knife only in so far as it is unequivocally a tool and not a weapon. In the home, that means in the kitchen; in the abattoir, it means in the tripe-dressing room, on the pig line, or even (in the rarest of cases) flaying bovines, but never for bleeding itself.

[3] It is important to recognise that there are exceptions. For example, the woman who won first prize in a flaying competition will certainly have had to bleed the animal that she dressed. However, one would need precise information about her access to the trade, the conditions in which she practised it, and so on.

47 The lamb line: general view of a double line

With the exception of the punchers and the man who hangs the lambs up on the two carousels, all the slaughtermen stand outside the lines to perform machine-flaying, evisceration, and finishing.

According to a well-known analysis (Tabet 1979, pp. 5–61), men universally dispossessed women of tools, particularly weapons, in order to reduce them to their bodies alone. However, it looks as if the examples on which the author based her thesis could be better explained in terms of the object of the ban having been not the weapons themselves but very precisely *killing by bloodshed*. Outside marriage and/or in the absence of men, women may hunt and fish. Marriage, however, excludes them from these activities. The incompatibility of hunting and marriage is undoubtedly to be seen as an

11 'SHE COULDN'T DO IT . . . SHE WOULDN'T DO IT'

'Me and my sister, there were the two of us women . . . But she didn't do what I did. She did gut-dressing but not slaughtering, she couldn't do that.'

'Why not?'

'Because she had a thing about touching animals, she was terrified of hurting an animal. She couldn't do it! I used to tell her: "But it's a job! It isn't . . . I don't hurt them." She wouldn't do it. She wouldn't do it, didn't like it. Whereas flaying heads, doing guts, all that she enjoyed. But to go and fetch an animal . . . She was frightened of animals, to start with . . . '

'Even of sheep?'

'Of the lot! She just didn't like it.'

48 Large bovines

Animals enter the stunning race in single file. Visible in the background are the 'trap' and the hoisting and bleeding stations.

49 The empty ' trap' viewed from inside the race

After a flight of gently rising steps designed to encourage the animal forward, a shutter descends vertically to form the rear door of the 'trap', cutting the animal off from the one behind it and shutting it in. After stunning, the left wall of the 'trap' swings out and the animal slumps down on the concrete floor. The two side openings in the foreground are of course closed when the 'trap' is in operation.

50 An animal in the 'trap'

Visible on the left is the concrete ramp from which a man will stun the animal. The compressed-air pistol hangs within easy reach, the handle wrapped in hessian to give a better grip. It will be applied to the forehead of the animal, and by pressing the trigger the operator will effect perforation of the cranium by means of a captive bolt. The animal will then collapse inside the 'trap' as the man activates the tipping movement of the far wall.

incompatibility between the blood of life and the blood of death, so that the two opposing symbolic qualities of blood are divided between women and men. Women are not in fact forbidden either to kill, provided that bloodshed is not involved, or to shed blood, provided that the animal in question is already dead; moreover, they have access to the tools/weapons that those jobs require. The most consistent prohibition, according to Tabet herself, applies to throwing weapons, that is to say weapons that can kill only by inflicting a mortal wound, by spilling all the blood of the victim hit while still alive. So it is very much as if the object of the prohibitions were to remove the consubstantial ambiguity from blood and in particular from the spilling of blood, to separate the bloodshed that occasions death from the spilling of life. Put forward on the basis of observation of an abattoir (Vialles 1984), this hypothesis would not appear to be called into question by the discovery of a small number of women working in slaughterhalls. Not only that, but it receives powerful backing from the work of Françoise Héritier ([1979b] 1984–5) and, more recently, A. Testard (1986).

The fact remains that, in our societies, women do quite often kill animals by spilling their blood. For example, it has traditionally been women who kill farmyard animals for the family to eat. Granted, they usually stun the animal first; yet that in no way differs from the methods used in abattoirs, where, however, women do not perform bleeding. The most crucial difference seems instead to lie in the species of animal concerned: bleeding a hen or a rabbit is

51 Hoisting large bovines

As the previous animal, having been bled, is about to disappear behind the partition separating the 'trap' from animals heading towards the slaughterhall, a winch descends from the overhead track; a chain is passed round one of the animal's hind legs, the hitching plate is engaged in the hooks of the winch, and the animal is winched up on to the handling rail.

52 Bleeding

When it reaches the corner the animal is bled by making a broad incision in the carotid artery above the drain grating.

53 Flaying large bovines

The animal on the right has been partly flayed. For the flaying of the flanks, the suspended animal is steered between height-adjustable platforms on which two men stand to perform the flaying with the aid of strimmers. The animal on the left has been flayed and is leaving this station as the other arrives. Two strimmers are suspended within the men's reach.

'not the same', slaughterers will regularly reply when asked. So there are not only different kinds of blood but different kinds of animal. It is a whole complex of representations concerning animals and humans and men and women that is at issue here and that a simple study of abattoirs does not, at least for the moment, enable us to elucidate satisfactorily.

We must be content for the time being to note that the exclusion of women from certain jobs is due to something more than their possibly being granted a uniformly subordinate status; it has to do with a very much more complex pattern of symbolism – and one to which women adhere, since even when they are in a position to go against the usual procedure they do not do so. The bloody killing of large mammals is definitely men's work. And those men form a hierarchy according to their skill at handling the tool that is first of all the killing weapon, namely the knife. By the same token, they place animals in a hierarchy according to the degree of skill with the knife that is required to flay them. Moreover, none of this excludes the possibility of such a hierarchisation encountering others stemming from different sources (stockbreeders, consumers, theories of animality, etc.) but tending in the same direction.

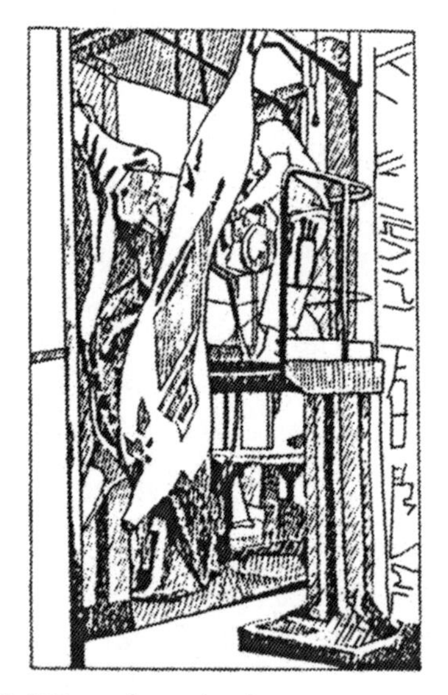

54 Splitting a large bovine

Using his right foot, the man controls the descent of the platform as he saws down through the carcass. Throughout the operation the heavy saw is suspended from a cable, which pays out as the operator presses down. The head, which is left attached to one of the sides, is separated from the other with a knife.

The 'trap'

This hierarchisation of men and animals with its parallel differentiation on both sides is tending to disappear in the process of planned modernisation. The constant refrain of abattoir managers, as it is of slaughterers of long standing, is that levels of skill are in decline. The fact is that young slaughterers have never even heard of some of the old practices, notably the art of 'presentation', once the height of mastery of the trade. Plans (still at the research stage in the region under consideration, but more advanced elsewhere) to introduce multi-use slaughter lines further emphasise this standardisation of men and animals.

Multi-use operation or polyvalency may be achieved in two ways, the second of which as it were rounds off the first. In the first place, it may take the form of installing plant capable of being adapted for the dressing of all so-called 'butchery' species (i.e., excluding pigs, except for the purposes of bleeding and evisceration); such plant will in particular comprise height-adjustable working platforms, the flaying of each species remaining as it is now ('peeling' for bovines, 'punching' for ovines). But it may also take the more radical form of altering traditional flaying methods in the direction of a generalised method of removing hides by pulling; and when all species are

55 Towards the weighing and cooling rooms

The pig carcasses on the left and the large bovines on the right, ready for weighing, are reflected in the freshly washed floor.

pulled, distinctions between men according to their degree of skill will inevitably disappear. Job fragmentation on the slaughter line appears to flow necessarily from the increased scale of slaughtering. So imperative is the process, in fact, that the actual numbers of animals being slaughtered are compounded by the standardisation of methods, further aggravating the mass effect.

So far, differentiations among species and among skills still remain, but there is already one point on which the effects of the standardisation of methods are becoming perceptible. We saw earlier (see above, pp. 43–4) how the 'trap' ['stunning pen' in English, but a literal translation of the French *piège* is used here for reasons that will become apparent] used for large bovines represents the epitome of 'rational' devices for restraining animals for the purposes of stunning. In the region studied here it is by no means the case that all species are dealt with in this way. Nevertheless, the 'trap' merits attention because it is located at a critical moment of the slaughtering process and because it is a standardising procedure without, however, impinging too significantly on skills. It supplies as it were an outline of a logical development that has not yet reached its conclusion, though its point of insertion in the chain of operations gives it its full significance.

The principal effect of the 'trap' is to do away with what one author calls 'the brief death struggle' (Gascar 1973, p. 124), in which man, at some risk to himself, pits himself against beast. In the 'trap', by contrast, the animal is held apart from the man, who is then able to slaughter it in complete safety, even if various minor incidents may still occur. This obvious contrast already reveals the higher determination of the term 'trap', which is used constantly in everyday speech and occasionally even in technical documents. Traps contrast with combat as cunning, ambush, and treason contrast with war and fair hunting, where there is some risk on both sides, however unequally apportioned.

According to one authority (Jamin 1979, pp. 22–9), ceptological activity (trapping) is distinguished from cynegetic activity (hunting) in that the trap, which is designed for one species and one environment, functions in the absence of man ('maximum distance between the hunter and his prey') with the help of a decoy and bait. Furthermore, the aim of trapping is to catch wild animals, often without bloodshed (at least, bloodshed is not necessarily involved). These characteristics of trapping and hunting can usefully be compared with those of the 'trap' in which animals are slaughtered: the 'trap' is designed for a species, albeit a domestic species; operator and animal are separated, so far as is possible in the circumstances; the result is certain and not subject to chance, as is the case when ceptological activity is directed against wild species or when the hunter pursues game.

Wild or domestic animal, whether considered as species or individual, the presence or absence of man – all these things lend themselves to analysis in terms of physical, social, and symbolic distance between man and animal.

Wildness and domestication represent different degrees of distance between men and animals. Wildness in the animal kingdom is the exact opposite of human civility, while domestication brings the animal into the human group and so humanises it, however slightly. Between themselves, however, they are opposed; they form two contrasting states of animality over against humanity.

In relations between man and a species, the individual animal remains at a distance, an anonymous object of man's indifference. The individualised relationship, on the other hand, involves recognition by man of a particular creature, and in this respect hunting evokes anthropomorphism as vigorously as do relationships with pets: in making the animal either an enemy or a friend, both relationships establish a kind of common nature between men and animals, a relationship on an equal footing, be it in the shared risk of the chase or in ordinary everyday life. Hunted animals may be given names or nicknames just like dogs and cats (e.g., the old lion dubbed 'The American' in J. Rouch's 1965 documentary film *La chasse au lion à l'arc*), and both the former and the latter are credited with feelings, thoughts, and various qualities, just like human beings.

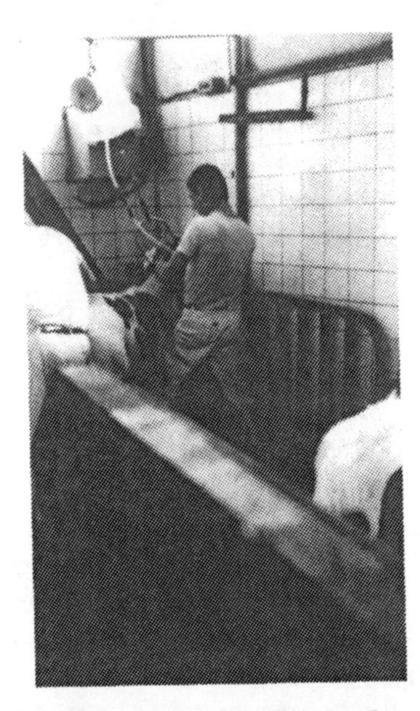

56 The calf line: immobilisation and stunning

57 The calf line: entering the slaughterhall

After bleeding and a period of draining-out, the calves enter the slaughterhall. Their heads and feet will be removed immediately.

58 The calf line: flaying the hindquarters

The right hind thigh is being flayed with the aid of a strimmer, the animal having been suspended by its left hind leg. It will then be suspended by its flayed right hock while the left hind leg is opened up and the hock flayed. Finally, the animal will be suspended by both hocks for the flaying of the left thigh.

So a distinction needs to be drawn between domestication for the purposes of food, which concerns species, and domestication for other purposes, which singularises individuals.[4] It may be remarked in this connection that, traditionally, animals raised for the family to eat are not individualised by giving them a name. A herd of cows may all have names, but they are not destined for the table. On the other hand, calves that are raised for sale as meat remain

[4] The 'food' I am referring to here is of course meat, so that 'domestication for food purposes' should be understood primarily as the exploitation of animals for the consumption of their flesh. Consequently, 'domestication for non-food purposes' does not exclude the extraction of foodstuffs (e.g. milk) from the live animal; simply, it does not have as its object the slaughter of the animal in order to provide food in the form of meat. From this standpoint, working animals occupy a somewhat ambiguous intermediate position between 'food' animals and pets. They might, for the sake of brevity, be referred to as 'working pets', to distinguish them from 'leisure pets'. Social and economic conditions have a great deal to do with the distinction between working pets and leisure pets. However, raising animals purely for meat appears to exclude any possibility of making pets of them. It follows that we can retain, as the two poles of this opposition, on the one hand domestication for food and on the other hand domestication for pleasure (even if the object is man's pleasure more than that of the animal!).

Once again, we find ourselves here at the heart of a complex system of relationships to animals and of representations that have yet to be analysed in greater detail. Looking at abattoirs provides a glimpse of what is involved, but to elaborate on this would take us far beyond the scope of the present study.

59 The calf line: abdominal evisceration following flaying of hindquarters.

anonymous. Similarly, pigs, hens, and rabbits are never given names, and if they do happen to receive one it excludes them *ipso facto* from being eaten. 'You don't eat something that has a name,' says a character in Bill Forsyth's film *Local Hero* (1984), discovering to his horror that a 'baptised' rabbit has been served up in a stew. The fact that, in France, pigs are often called 'Monsieur' ['Sir'] is no exception since, quite apart from the fact that this is a title rather than a name, the pun involved in the allusion to a pig's being *vétu de soie(s)* [the French word *soie* meaning both 'pig bristle' and 'silk'] ironically suggests a kind of class cannibalism. Man's relationship to wild animals may thus be either a species relationship or an individual relationship (trapping or hunting). Similarly, domestication does not in itself imply an individual relationship; it may not go beyond the species relationship.

Finally, man's degree of actual proximity is a further indicator of the distance (physical, this time) between men and animals. Trapping offers an instance of the distance from wild animals constituting a maximum, while hunting is an illustration of that same distance being at a minimum. The proximity of domestic animals is modified in accordance with the two degrees of the species relationship and the individual relationship. The ratio between the distances from the two kinds of domestic animal is thus very similar to the ratio between the distances from the two kinds of wild animal: trapping/hunting = domestication for food/domestication for pleasure (i.e., not for food), a formula that can be read as an equality of ratios or as a progression whose two mean terms are equal.

This can be summed up as follows:

activities \ characteristics	W	S	D	R	DB
TRAPPING	+	+	++	–	–
HUNTING	+	–	–	–	+
DOMESTICATION (for food)	–	+	–	+	+
DOMESTICATION (for pleasure)	–	–	– –	+	–

W: wildness (+)/domestication (–)
S: species relationship (+)/individual relationship (–)
D: physical distance, maximum (++)/minimum (– –)
R: result of action, certain (+)/chance (–)
DB: death by bloodshed (+)/absence of bloodshed (–)

What this shows is that the first two columns by themselves determine the content of the others. The wildness of the animal and the individuation of the relationship to it define:

1 physical distance, as their logical conjunction $(W . S)$
2 certainty of the result, as the negation of wildness $(\bar{W})$
3 the spilling of blood, as their exclusive disjunction $(W \wedge S)$

The spilling of blood thus corresponds to the mean distances when characteristics W and S are opposites and cancel each other out, either because individuation reduces the distance separating man from the wild animal (hunting), or because the species relationship distends the proximity to the domesticated animal. Extreme distances rule out bloodshed. Not too far, not too near – the ethnologist recognises this search for the right distance, whether in marriage choices or in hostilities, halfway between complete identity and the kind of radical difference that, by excess or by default ('excess of identical' or excess of difference; Gomez da Silva 1983, 1984; Héritier 1979a, 1985b), tips over into the absolute where, by definition, exchange is no longer possible. So the spilling of blood, particularly for the purposes of obtaining food, certainly comes into the sphere of exchanges, in the middle zone where passages, ambiguities, and reversals are possible, in the zone of relativity and of relationships, where steps need to be taken to preserve or to re-establish what Françoise Héritier has called the 'balance of opposites' (Héritier 1979b, 1981).

However, in the 'trap' in the abattoir (which fully constitutes a trap, since no animal can emerge from it alive), this balanced exchange is upset.

60 The calf line: flaying of flanks and forequarters

Suspended by its rear hocks, the carcass is slung 'hammock-fashion' by hooks inserted in the forelegs to facilitate flaying of the flanks and forequarters. The hide will be left attached by a strip several centimetres wide down the middle of the back, then pulled off by traction once the carcass has been returned to the vertical position. The next step is evisceration of the chest cavity.

In hunting, clearly the exchange manifests itself in the confrontation between man and animal, a confrontation in which both share the risks (or the chances), a fair fight, a fight between equals (symbolically, at least). The indignant condemnation that greets any kind of 'fixed' hunting (hunting made easy) confirms this. Hunting is tolerable when it has something of the appearance of an equal combat with the animal concerned, whereby the hunter deserves his game and is not indulging in some vile 'butchery'.

In traditional domestication for food purposes, the exchange tends instead to take the form of an individual or collective contract (just as the combat involved in hunting may be individual or collective[5]). Take the individual contract first, the one between man and an animal. Feeding and looking after an animal gives a man a right to its flesh. The eater thus legitimises his eating of meat by virtue of the care and attention he has bestowed on the animal, in slaughtering which he is, as it were, realising his investment. But this kind of traditional domestic slaughtering is also accompanied by festive exchanges.

[5] The collective character of the combat does not imply a relationship to the animal *species* as such, this being a category of thought rather than a collection of individuals.

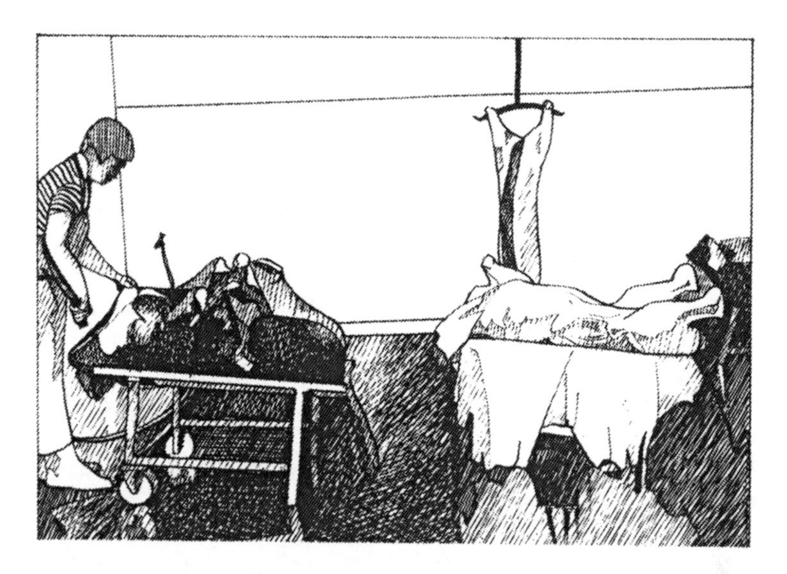

61 Dressing calves on cradles.

Left: the four feet, partially cut, are tied together in pairs by interlacing the tendons. This is to facilitate opening-up by placing the muscles under tension. Right: as the carcass is flayed, the hide hangs down over the bench like a cloth. Background: a carcass ready for weighing hangs from a cambrel.

Everyone 'kills *the* pig' (i.e., his own, the one he has fed and earned), but the sharing with neighbours and relations (even if more symbolically than actually equal) incorporates the individual man/animal contract in a collective contract among men, whereby each person is indirectly in touch with the animal species considered in its entirety. Investing in his own animal has given him credit in the form of an entitlement to other, similar animals fed by other men.

By contrast, in industrial slaughtering there is no longer, thanks to the 'trap', either combat or contract. There is no combat because that is precisely what the 'trap' is designed to eliminate; by facilitating the handling and slaughter of animals, particularly the larger ones, it avoids direct confrontation as well as the possibility of accidents or acts of violence. There is no contract because the person who slaughters the animal has no other relationship with it than which exists at the moment of death. He is not killing an animal he has fed himself but a series of animals on a production line, and he is doing it for money. 'I tell people I'm a hired killer,' slaughterers will say jokingly, 'I'm paid to kill.' If there is still a contract here it is of a quite different kind, involving the animal purely as an object, just like the victim of a criminal 'contract'.

This rupture of any kind of symbolic contract with the animal is further aggravated by the fact that the objects of this large-scale slaughter are 'working pets' (see this chapter, n. 4), namely large bovines. Killing a 'cull' bull or cow may be a necessity to which the owner resigns him/herself for want of a better alternative. Sacrificing a fine animal as part of a festive occasion may take on the appearance of a rendering wild in 'the brief combat of death' or alternatively an act of consent on the part of the animal itself. Necessity, the assumption or provocation of wildness, consent – any one of these may lend an appearance of legitimacy to the slaughter of an animal. But the serial slaughter of large bovines imprisoned in the 'trap' is in a confused way seen as an abuse of domestication, the revelation of a sort of hidden clause in a contract that seemed to represent a simple exchange of services.

This is clearly apparent in the general feeling of repugnance attached to the slaughter of horses and even in the separate position occupied by horse butchers [*chevalins*] within the butchery trade. Even if, as in the case of large bovines, the horse's actual role has changed considerably (and, since the Second World War, very rapidly), it is still, in terms of the way in which it is represented, a working as well as a leisure companion. People have qualms about slaughtering horses, and some slaughterers will in fact refuse to do so. A horse in the 'trap' is the supreme betrayal, as if this animal ought, because of 'the bi-lateral pact between the horse family and homo sapiens' (Lizet 1975, p. 341), to receive either a humane or a sacrificial death but not be the object of industrial slaughter.

The 'trap' could be said to place the animal too far from or too close to man. Too close, because this is still a domestic animal and because the 'trap' appears to abuse the ease with which it can therefore be approached. Too far, because the 'trap' dissolves the partial individuation acquired through

12 'HORSES ARE SACRED'

'I've never slaughtered horses. Oh no, not that! We didn't do it, anyway, because the butchery trade was very sharply divided, still is, as a matter of fact.'

'Was it because you wouldn't have wanted to, or did it just work out like that?'

'I wasn't in that line of work at the time. Later on, though, I wouldn't have slaughtered them because by then I'd become an old rider, so that was it so far as slaughtering horses was concerned. I don't even eat horseflesh. The reason is, I've come to love horses. I had an amazing horse in the army. So that was it, horses are sacred to me now. Man's noblest conquest! I didn't even like ... I always felt uneasy, seeing a horse killed. Because it's an intelligent animal, a horse, it knows what's going on, not like a bullock, bovines are stupid, generally speaking they're stupid, but the horse is intelligent, that's different! It knows it's about to die, you see its legs trembling. I didn't like seeing that. There were people who would slaughter them, I used not to watch. Afterwards, once they were on the ground being flayed, then I didn't mind. I didn't like to see a horse die, oh no, that I didn't like.'

domestication. It is certainly not by chance that the 'trap' was first used for large bovines and members of the horse family. Granted, their size and strength as well as the concern for worker safety amply justify its use. But one wonders whether it was not also an attempt to conceal a dubious legitimacy. The fact is that it turns out to have a perverse rationale. In order to avoid violent combat, it increases the distance between man and animal. Yet in so doing it increases the illegitimacy by dissolving any residual individuality as well as any kind of contractual dimension. By facilitating large-scale slaughter in complete security, it enhances culpability at the very point where it was supposed to remove culpability by eliminating risks and violent incidents. It is the end-result of the relatively recent massive increase in scale in a particular branch of slaughtering (that of large bovines and equines) at a time when representations of the animals concerned have not changed substantially.

A disturbing fraternity

In the absence of a 'trap', how are large bovines slaughtered? As we have seen (above, p. 54), a rope around the animal's neck or lashed to its horns is passed through a ring set in the floor; the pistol is applied to the forehead of the animal, which then collapses as soon as the captive bolt pierces its cranium. The job was more difficult when it had to be done with a poleaxe (see figure 22). Everyone with experience of this method of slaughtering (with neither 'trap' nor pistol) will speak of the dangers involved and describe how they themselves, sooner or later, were injured or obliged to flee from a maddened animal that had broken loose or suffered a 'miss'. The confrontation between man and animal was thus very much more dangerous than (thanks to the 'trap') it is today; above all, such descriptions of the dangers incurred are proffered with considerable complacency, as if to indicate that an element of combat conferred a certain fairness on the slaughter of these large animals. It is impossible to tell how much violence was in fact a real possibility in such circumstances, but some degree of violence was undoubtedly involved. And, irrespective of any moral or humanitarian consideration, that violence and/or that danger may be seen as an attempt to restore a measure of legitimacy to slaughtering, either by portraying the animals concerned as wild and violent or through the medium of a fight that is not without some risk for man.

The 'trap', however, makes combat of any kind impossible, while at the same time the law curbs all violence so far as animals are concerned. Some re-adjustment of the perverse rationality of the 'trap' is in fact looked for through the development of 'humane' measures in the treatment of animals. Since it is impossible to re-establish the balance of exchange in industrial slaughtering through combat or the appearance of combat with the animals concerned, there seems to be a belief that it can be re-established by introducing a new contract, as it were, between humanity and the animal kingdom. The humane measures involved do not extend to a renunciation of meat-eating, but they do seek to create an awareness of all creatures capable of feeling pain as sharing a common nature. In the context of slaughtering, they seek to legitimise the eating of the flesh of animals through the medium of man's gentleness towards them; the blood of animals is, so to speak, exchanged against the heart or good-heartedness of man. However, such a contract remains a highly abstract affair unless backed up by a psychology and a sensitivity that the occupational training [in French, the more direct *formation*] of abattoir personnel sets out to inculcate. At all events, there are some very dissuasive sanctions in this field, quite apart from the concern to produce high-quality meat, which good treatment helps to foster.

The preoccupation with 'humaneness' does not in fact originate in social circles familiar with animals:

> This movement did not begin among butchers, miners, or farmers whose work brought them into direct contact with animals ... It was closely bound up with the development of towns and the emergence of an industrial order that gave animals an increasingly marginal role in the production process. That industrial order appeared first in England, so it was there that concern for animals found the widest expression (Thomas 1983).

This 'new feeling' arose among 'members of the middle class who had little sympathy with the military traditions of the aristocracy', and it enabled them to campaign against cruel sports while at the same time exerting themselves to discipline the working classes. Thomas goes on:

> The 1835 law against cruelty to animals announced its intention of reducing both the suffering of dumb creatures and 'demoralisation of the people' ... The S.P.C.A. (Society for the Prevention of Cruelty to Animals) may thus be regarded as another middle-class movement aimed at civilising the lower classes.

The same author further observes:

> Love of animals was not often taken to the point where it would have threatened people's interests ... Most folk continued to exclude fish, beasts of prey, vermin, and insects. The requirements of human survival appeared to call for such an exclusion, just as they also, in practice, implicated certain sections of humanity.

That is not to say that farmers and butchers are uniformly cruel and pitiless (enlightened self-interest usually leads people to treat animals well, whether it is the best work they want to get out of them or the best meat). But they do distinguish clearly between men and animals. 'We draw a distinction between men and animals,' slaughterers will often tell you, partly to reject the images of violence attached to those who slaughter animals but partly also to denounce a lack of differentiation in universal kindness that is capable of animalising humans as much as it humanises animals. This declared difference is entirely compatible with a benevolent attitude towards animals and is the basis of the homologies between the two levels previously distinguished; the parallel hierarchies and the analogies employed unfold against the background of this initial separation.

Nevertheless, in stressing the common nature of men and animals as sentient creatures, the humanitarian concern may meet with agreement. It is readily acknowledged that animals are capable of feeling pain, and they are quite often credited with emotions and premonitions as well as sensory awareness. It is a limited agreement, however, and both the premisses and the consequences of the humane viewpoint with regard to animals are different. In this case it is a question of establishing a kind of contract of non-violence (a relative non-violence, because there is no renunciation of meat-eating) between men and animals; very specifically, it is a question of eliminating pain and consequently any kind of brutality.

Yet whereas the contract that belongs to domestication receives its authority from being an interpretation of a state of affairs, the contract of non-violence may be merely programmatical. Quite simply, it may be no more than a moral obligation. For if men share with their 'lesser brethren' the nature of sentient beings, that shared nature entails obligations for man alone – for the very reason that man is something more than a sentient being. It is the dignity of man that is at issue in kindness to animals, the struggle against Thomas's 'demoralisation'.

By establishing a link between men and animals, humane treatment of the latter appears to compensate for the effects of the 'trap', which eliminates both combat and the contract. However, as a mere abstract moral requirement, the link does not go in the other direction as well, namely from animal to man. It merely unites man with himself, by virtue of his relationship to animals but as it were over their heads. In the day-to-day business of slaughtering, all that is left so far as man is concerned is the strangeness of slaughtering 'lesser brethren' on a massive scale and at no risk to himself. By treating animals 'humanely', man is in fact humanising them, and by the same token the feeling of unease increases in proportion to the taxonomical ambiguity created by dissolving the frontiers between humanity and animality. In the principle of the 'trap', mechanics and humaneness do not in the last resort compensate for each other, leaving the human mind confused and at a loss in the face of the job to be done. The situation is comparable to that of the invention of the guillotine: a nice, neat, dignified machine 'will prevent executions from potentially becoming "a struggle and a massacre"' (Arasse 1982–3, p. 124), in the words of executioner Sanson, setting out the 'views of humanity' that must lead to the adoption of the new mechanical decapitator.

All this helps to explain why slaughterers will stress the risks they run at the slaughter station. Various incidents may indeed occur during stunning, suspension, and bleeding as the animals' bodies are thrown about by their reflex movements. But the danger does not appear to be much greater than that of receiving a wound at any of the other workstations. When one man does both stunning and bleeding, he will often mention the isolation of the slaughter station, which would delay the discovery of any accident that might occur. While the 'trap' would seem to guarantee maximum safety for the men concerned, those men will nevertheless lay claim to an element of risk, and the reason is undoubtedly that, in industrial slaughtering, risk reintroduces an appearance of fairness, which offsets the facile treachery of the 'trap'.

In the absence of any trace of an equitable contract, risk, whether real or imagined, is a better recourse than the decidedly disturbing feeling of fraternity with the sentient being that is to be slaughtered. It is a highly complex system of relationships and representations that operates here, and one that, being closely interwoven with actual practice, is capable of legitimising (or at least making acceptable) the slaughter of animals for human consumption.

Unless, possibly, the industrial dimension has inflicted such deep damage on acquired logics that it will take a long time for these to reconstruct themselves?

CONCLUSION

The first conclusion to be drawn from this study is, as it happens, the impossibility of drawing any conclusion. There is still material to be worked on, and it will probably involve some reorganisation of the analyses outlined here. Abattoirs offer a preliminary outing (not excluding others) by which we may seek to answer the initial question concerning our food, particularly that part of it which is of animal origin. We see now that this question needs to organise a logical ensemble too huge to be seen clearly and reconstructed at one go. Everything that is unsatisfactory, hesitant, or limited about the present work indicates the directions in which research still needs to be undertaken. For the moment, then, we must be content with a 'sub-total'.

In the first place, one thing that can be said is that (remembering the Ethnological Heritage Department's overall brief of 'popular naturalist skills') slaughtering tends to be a somewhat 'unpopular' subject: no one wants to know about it, except of course those who are professionally involved and to whom knowledge of the subject is consequently restricted. The separation of slaughtering from butchery and the associated banishment of abattoir premises have contributed greatly towards keeping that knowledge between narrow bounds. The network of official regulations and standards has completed the process by clothing a complex body of practical knowledge in a prescriptive discourse that leaves everything it does not legitimise in the shadows. A kind of esoterism that is not necessarily transgressive becomes almost automatically entrenched beneath those regulations and standards, from where it is not easy to flush it out, even if it is not deliberately being kept secret.

This is why it is particularly important here for the investigator patiently to win the confidence of the slaughterers. As elsewhere, he/she has to be able to reach beyond the initial stereotyped discourse, going behind the answers that are intended for external consumption (to satisfy the curiosity of the outsider) and at the same time serve to close ranks. Yet to an even greater extent than elsewhere, perhaps, the investigator needs to become invisible, as it were, allowing people's behaviour to approximate as closely as possible to what it would have been had no investigator been present. However, he/she is always more visible than might be thought, and the interplay of relationships with the investigator has its own significance. The whole complex field of the relationship to the 'subject' is involved here, of course, together with all the epistemological problems that it comprises and that are the most constant unspoken factor in the discipline. But in the same way as the 'subjects' of the study no doubt convey more than they think (or different things), the investigator, even as he/she seeks to be objective, is certainly not in control of everything – nor should be, possibly?

The second piece of evidence to emerge from this study is the absence of any regional peculiarity in terms of discourses and practices. Given the impossibility of making any exact comparison with other regions so far as the practice of slaughtering is concerned, it would be unwise to draw any definite conclusions. The standardising effect of regulations certainly contributes towards homogenising the phenomenon to which they are applied. But it is also entirely possible that, even before regulations were introduced, there were no significant differences in the ways in which animals were slaughtered for meat. After all, a long cultural tradition holds that only those animals may be eaten that have been killed by the hand of man and the shedding of blood. That leaves little room for variation, except in terms of circumstantial detail and the precise methods employed, concerning which we lack information.

The only precise element of comparison was found in Georges Franju's film, *The Slaughterhouse*. The bleeding of calves by total decapitation shown in the film regularly provoked disapproval among slaughterers. But what conclusion can be drawn from one isolated element, the range of which we do not know? All we can do is record the fact for possible future comparisons, noting at the same time the absence of internal diversity in the region studied. For be they Basque or Gascon, natives of Béarn, Lomagne, or Marsan, the people of the region go about slaughtering and dressing animals for meat in much the same way.

Differences do exist, on the other hand, in what comes after slaughtering. In general terms, we know that there are regional variations in the way in which carcasses are cut up, even if the so-called 'Parisian' method is the dominant one. From a different standpoint, attention has been drawn to the variety of names applied to the various parts of animals and carcasses (Fossat 1971). And as regards the use of blood in cooking, my fieldwork enabled me to collect several recipes using blood and offering some interesting variations. However, none of that directly concerns slaughtering.

Lastly, the industrial character of slaughtering today appears to challenge a number of traditional representations, both as regards the work of slaughtering itself and as regards animals and meat. Whichever way we look at this change, it has to be noted that it calls for a reconsideration on everyone's part of our relationships to animals and our attitudes to their slaughter. Here too what is at issue is probably 'the secret springs of all social life, as well as certain of its conditions that may be regarded as essential', with the result that we must 'accept that deeper reasons of a social and moral nature maintain the number of individuals called to live together within limits between which lies what might be termed the population optimum' (Levi-Strauss 1983, p. 381). Similar reasons may also be at work in determining the number of animals 'called' to die in order to provide food, meaning that we should need to find out what symbolic logic nourishes the roots of the sensibility that feels the need to place limits on the mass slaughter of animals.

Even if not all the information collected has been systematically exploited here, we have caught glimpses of various aspects, each of which has its own intrinsic interest. To conclude, let us confine ourselves to listing the few acquisitions capable of suggesting an answer to our initial question: what is meat?

To begin with (and this stems directly from slaughtering by bleeding), meat is neither the animal nor even the corpse of the animal. De-animation, which consists in removing the *anima* or vital principle, results in a bloodless body that is the only thing that may be prepared for human consumption as food.

That bloodless body is, furthermore, de-animalised. This is the significance of dressing, which literally consists in stripping the body of its animality. The carcass obtained in this way no longer has anything to do with the animal from which it has in a sense been extracted. It is a foodstuff, a *substance*; all the links that attached it to a once living body have been severed. In particular, that substance has been separated from everything too obviously reminiscent of the animal itself: the hide that enveloped it, the excrement that crudely testified to its active physiology, the various bits of offal suggestive both of the shape of the animal and its former organic unity.

In focusing on the slaughterhall, we have paid little attention to offal and the processing of offal, which takes place elsewhere. But the reader will have noted that, in defining the various kinds of offal, Chaudieu relates them to the animal rather than to the carcass (see above, ch. 4, n. 1), and that they are usually distinguished from meat, whether to place them above or below it in status. It is perhaps through offal that we might best distinguish between two logics with regard to meat: a 'zoophagan' logic, favoured by those who like to acknowledge the living in what they are eating and who consequently rate offal especially highly, notably the kinds in which a particular virtue of the living creature is felt to be concentrated (liver, primarily, but also brains, sweetbreads, marrow, and testicles); and what etymological symmetry requires us to call a 'sarcophagan' logic, cultivated by those who will only consent to consume an abstract substance, in which nothing can be traced back to the animal, and who therefore shun offal in disgust as too obviously betraying the origin of what they are eating. But it would require a more sophisticated analysis of practices and vocabulary and of the relationships between the various kinds of offal and certain animals slaughtered for food (pigs, the preparation of which closely resembles that of white offal, but also poultry, which are often left whole and so remain identifiable until they reach the table) to define with rigour the place of offal and of each species of animal eaten in the system of our meat-eating.

We do not, after all, eat just any animals. Exclusive carnivores, particularly carrion-eaters, are not on the list. Aquatic animals are not looked upon as furnishing meat. Birds and rabbits do not fall within the category of so-called 'butcher's meat'. The flesh of animals seems in fact to be hierarchised according to the particular animal's habitat. Those that live in or beside water are not meat at all; those that can fly or live above or below ground appear to constitute an intermediate category; 'true' meat comes from four-footed animals, exclusive herbivores, domesticated ruminants – in other words, the animals with which in the most tangible sense we live on an equal footing, as it were, the animals of which we are able to consume the milk of reproductive females, or the flesh, but not the blood, of specimens that have been fattened up.

Confining ourselves to the everyday terms, we eat beef [*boeuf*], veal [*veau*], mutton [*mouton*], lamb [*agneau*] – and pork [*porc*], but here we leave the pig to one side, having seen what a problematical animal is this '*bête singulière*', as one authority calls it (Fabre-Vassas 1982). The French terms specifically omit the females of the species. Yet among calves and lambs, not only males are present; females that have become unfit for breeding are also slaughtered and eaten, having first, so far as possible, been fattened up for the purpose. Finally, this vocabulary likewise makes no mention of reproductive male animals. We are considered to eat only young (and hence as it were asexual) animals and castrated or 'cull' adults, that is to say animals that are excluded from genetic activity, whether as being, so to speak, not up to it or beyond it.

Castration, we know, is thought to promote fattening:

> Usually two reasons are put forward for the castration of domestic animals. The first, which is a valid reason, is that a castrated animal is more docile. The second, which I am assured possesses no scientific validity, is that a castrated animal produces tastier meat in a shorter time (Leach 1964).

Yet it is the second reason that is decisive and accounts for the practice of castrating animals destined for slaughter. A veterinary officer and meat department inspector writing in 1880 accepted as fact 'the positive effect so far as fattening is concerned of annihilating the genetic orgasm' (Baillet 1880, p. 7); 'experience shows,' he goes on, that a castrated animal 'benefits at an earlier stage of the fattening process from the food it is given' (*ibid.*,

p. 85). Similarly, Chaudieu notes that 'there exists a prejudice against cow meat', whereas what he calls *taures* ('female bovines that have never calved') 'are much sought-after for the delicacy of their meat' (Chaudieu 1970, pp. 147, 139). Fattening and reproductive activity are thus seen as mutually exclusive.

This is what gives the prejudice according to which castration promotes fattening its full significance. In this part of France (as, it would seem, virtually all over the world) it is widely thought that food turns into blood and blood into milk or sperm, depending on the degree of coction that it undergoes in a male or female body (Héritier 1985c). In fact 'the nature of the food affects the quality of the semen' (Héritier 1985a, p. 61) but also of the whole body, including the flesh. These transformations must operate in other mammals to the same extent as they do in humans. It follows logically that a barren cow is incapable of turning blood into milk, that a castrated animal is rendered incapable of turning blood into sperm, and that a sexually immature animal is as yet unable to do either. Since all such animals are believed to fatten better, what this means is that when blood is turned neither into milk, nor into sperm, it is turned into fat. An animal that is sexually active loses sperm or milk, both of which are quintessences of blood; if it is sexually inactive, it conserves the relevant quintessence, reinvesting it in its own body in the form of fat. Castrating an animal therefore means artificially steering the alchemy of the blood in the direction of fat rather than in that of sperm or milk. It follows that fat (which will be eaten) is the equivalent, in the alimentary register, of sperm or blood in the genetic register. Correlatively, eating fat or meat that is 'marbled' or permeated with fat is the same as eating a quintessence of blood.

This does not contradict the requirement for meat to be bloodless. The blood that is spilled is blood that has not been quintessentialised, the vital minimum. By contrast, blood that has been quintessentialised is seen as a surplus precisely because it has been invested beyond the mere survival of the organism. To shed blood and not eat it is to bar oneself access to minimal individual life; to eat fat or fat meat is to fortify oneself with a surplus of life, of which the stoutness of the slaughtered animal constitutes visible proof.

Two comments may lend further weight to this line of argument. In the *langue d'Oc*, the same word (*meula*) serves both for 'marrow' and for 'fat' or 'stoutness'. If it is true that 'sperm and marrow are of the same nature' (Héritier 1985b, p. 121) and that both, like fat, are quintessences of blood, it is easy to understand how the same word can cover both marrow and fat, denoting that which in the body (be it human or animal) represents the stockpiling of a rich surplus of life. On the other hand, the vocabulary of [French] butchery includes the word *amourette*: 'the spinal marrow of slaughter animals is commonly referred to by this name. In some regions it also denotes the testicles of the young bull or of young rams, which are edible and often in great demand' (Chaudieu 1970, p. 21). (In the latter case, of course, the plural is used, *amourettes*, or alternatively – though according to one informant only – *la cervelle d'en-bas* [perhaps 'the brain between the legs'].) *Amourette* is certainly a suggestive term and one that further underlines the semantic blur between marrow and sperm. Altogether, there does appear to be a linguistic and symbolic continuity (blood/sperm or milk, sperm or milk/marrow, marrow/fat) enabling us to regard fat as a metamorphosis of blood.

Finally, as regards wild animals too, the alimentary and sexual quintessences of blood are mutually exclusive. Male game animals, as we know, are castrated as soon as they have been killed, on the principle that the flesh of an uncastrated animal would be inedible, possessing a bad taste (Fabre-Vassas 1982). Now, if the blood of an 'entire' animal is normally transformed into sperm, castration immediately following bleeding consists in separating the sexual quintessence from the edible substance; castration completes bleeding, the latter getting rid of the vital principle, the former eliminating its sexual metamorphosis. The result is an exclusively alimentary substance, without interference from the sexual dimension.

This would mean that, so far as animals are concerned, the food-producing and sexual functions are mutually exclusive. This is probably not unrelated to the fact that cooking, particularly in cultures that place a high value on fat meat, is the exclusive province of women of child-bearing age, i.e. neither pre-pubescent nor post-menopausal:

> While a powerful feminine complicity is developed in this gynaeceum kitchen, each women also has assigned to her there, *in accordance with her position in the genealogical network* and in the mechanics of kinship, her very status within the family: there are those who peel the vegetables and wash the dirty utensils and those who prepare the dishes with the food that the others have got ready for use. In other words, some women are at the heart of the culinary operation, while others are kept on the side-lines. What we have here is a real division of labour. *The grandmothers and daughters* do the peeling and are *no more than helpers*. They assist and observe; all they do is 'pass the salt'. For the daughters, it is a question of learning. The grandmothers, who a generation earlier were pressuring their daughters-in-law to reproduce the culinary heritage, are now reduced to the status of assisting with a process that for a long time they controlled. As for the *mothers*, the generation in between, they are *the repositories of the knowledge, commanding the culinary process* [N.V.'s emphasis]; with regard to their mothers-in-law, they are making up for their former submission; with regard to their daughters, they are handing down not merely the culinary knowledge but also an image of motherhood that shall determine the relationship of alliance and dominance between mother and daughter (Bahloul 1983, pp. 193–4)

No one will fail to recognise in this description a distribution of family roles, albeit variously stressed. Nor could anyone fail to see that the real cooks, the proper cooks, are women of child-bearing age, the ones who have knowledge and command of every sort of coction, that of children as well as that of food (and above all meat), the ones who know about the

62 The butcher's trade, nineteenth century (Grube Arch, Bonn Abb)
Plate from Nagel, Schipf, and Frentz, *L'Art et la viande* ('Art and meat'), Paris, Erti, 1984.

things of the belly [the French word *ventre* covering both 'stomach' and 'womb'].

To return to abattoirs, the presence of women in the tripe-dressing room now takes on a fresh significance, fitting into a coherent symbolic whole. Logically, a job described in French as *faire les ventres* (i.e., the work of cleaning and preparing the stomachs and intestines used for tripe) could only fall to them. And if men have largely supplemented women here, this could only happen as machines have been brought in to do most of the work; in other words, it came when an intermediate element separated them from the material they were dealing with, while at the same time providing some technological compensation for the indignity of such work.

To recapitulate, then, domestic animals (but also game) alternately serve either reproductive or alimentary goals, but never both at once. In this sense we can say that only animals that have 'had the chop' are ever eaten, whether the 'chop' is actual or symbolic in the sense that they are cut off from reproduction, permanently divided between breeders and food producers. Castration of animals that are to be fattened up is in itself an action on their blood, a drying-up of their sexual blood, as it were. Castration linked to bleeding pursues the same goal *in extremis*, namely preventing the spread or ebb of 'sexual blood' into meat destined for the table. In a word, complete bleeding is castrative bleeding. To say that we eat only bloodless flesh is to say also that we eat only meat that has been desexualised or 'neutered'. The consumption of certain kinds of offal, and *a fortiori* that of bulls from the bull-ring, provides inverse proof of this, for a person is then deliberately eating an organ or an animal believed to be endowed with enormous sexual power, not through any gastronomic partiality but by symbolic choice: he *knows* he is eating *toro*, which is to say active sexuality. However, the high incidence of distaste for this type of food suggests that choosing it is in some way transgressive, signifying the curious synthesis of the sexual and the alimentary. Ordinarily, that synthesis is accepted only when it is less in evidence (if the '*amourette*' is only marrow, a person can overlook what is going on). What we glimpse here is that the 'zoophagan' and 'sarcophagan' logics may have points of contact between them and that shifts in meaning provide a passage from one to the other.

Turning to the kitchen, we find a situation that is symmetrically reversed. Here the reproductive and the alimentary are linked in that it is the fertile women who do the cooking, particularly that of the most highly prized form of food, namely meat. However, they do not, as we have seen, do the slaughtering, at least not of livestock animals. So they cook exclusively meat that men have first 'cut' from the vital, reproductive dimension, making it neutral flesh. It is just as if a circle were being completed: men separate, on animals, human food from animal sexuality, while women perform, for

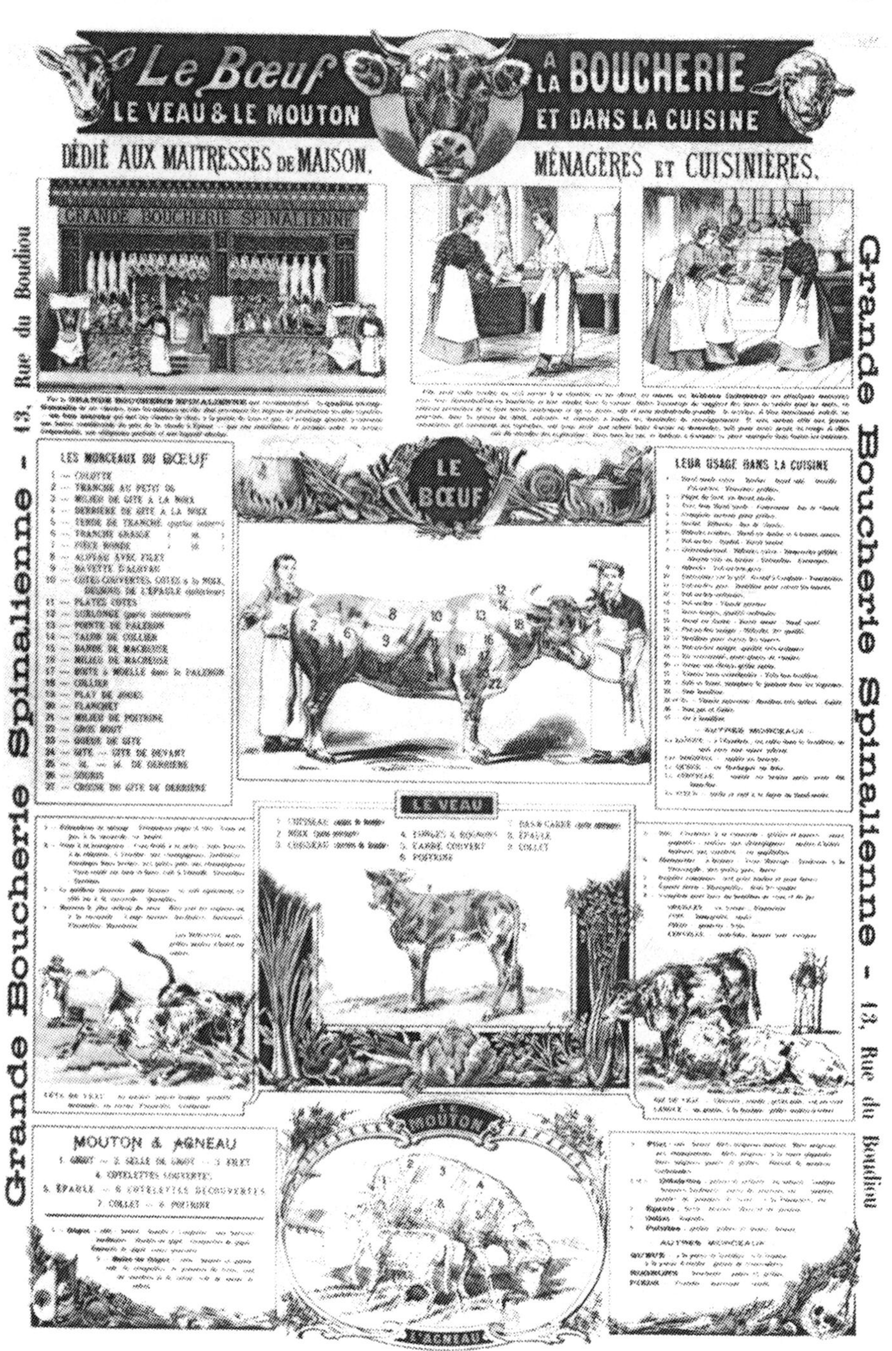

63 Plate from Pierre Gascar, *Les Bouchers* (see Gascar 1973, p. 115).

humans, the synthesis of human sexuality and food of animal origin. At the centre of the system is blood: blood that is made to flow, spilling *cru* and *cruel* (Latin: *cruor*, *crudus*); blood that is seen to flow and that can be cooked, spilling coctions of all kinds. If this view is correct, we see immediately how much it calls for more detailed development and how it can never, as it stands, be more than a hypothesis. At least it suggests that the study of abattoirs is not an end in itself but makes sense only in the context of a set of very much more complex questions.

REFERENCES

Agulhon, M., 1981, 'Le sang des bêtes: le problème de la protection des animaux en France au XIXe siècle', in *Romantisme* 31, pp. 81–109.

Arasse, D., 1982–3, 'La guillotine ou l'inimaginable "effet d'une simple méchanique"', in *Revue des sciences humaines* 186–7, pp. 123–44.

Ariès, P., 1977, *L'Homme devant la mort*, Paris (Le Seuil).

Aufrant, Billon, Gielfrich, *et al.*, 1974, *Hygiène de l'abattage des animaux de boucherie*, preface by M. Mathieu, head of veterinary services at the [French] Ministry of Agriculture, *Informations techniques des services vétérinaires* nos. 45–8.

Bahloul, J., 1983, *Le culte de la table dressée: rites et traditions de la table juive algérienne*, Paris (Métaillié/Centre national des lettres).

Baillet, L., 1880, *Traité de l'inspection des viandes de boucherie, considérée dans ses rapports avec la zootechnie, la médecine vétérinaire et l'hygiène publique*, second edition (revised, corrected, and expanded, with 58 illustrations in the text), Paris (Asselin).

Barrau, J., 1983, *Les hommes et leurs aliments: esquisse d'une histoire écologique et ethnologique de l'alimentation humaine*, Paris (Messidor/Temps actuels).

Barthes, Roland, 1954–6, *Mythologies*, second edition [first edition Paris (Le Seuil), 1957], Paris (Le Seuil), 1970.

1970, *L'empire des signes*, new edition, Paris (Flammarion), 1980.

Benoist, L., 1980, *Le compagnonnage et les métiers*, fourth edition, Paris (PUF).

Benveniste, Emile, 1966, 'Euphémismes anciens et modernes' [1949], in *Problèmes de linguistique générale*, I, Paris (Gallimard), pp. 308–14.

Bloch, O. and von Wartburg, W., 1932, *Dictionnaire étymologique de la langue française*, preface by A. Meillet, Paris (PUF).

Bochet, N., 1983, 'Le comportement des bovins: savoirs traditionnels et scientifiques', in *Ethnozootechnie* 32, pp. 122–39.

Bouchet, D., 1980, 'Du sang dans le béton', in *Le Monde*, 26 October, p. XIV.

Calvino, Italo, 1983, *Palomar*, Turin (Einaudi).

CEMAGREF (Centre nationale du machinisme agricole, du Génie rurale, des Eaux et Forêts), 1980, (meat technology division, Clermont-Ferrand group), *Récolte, prétraitement et stockage du sang à l'abattoir*, study no. 6, October.

1982a, *De la polyvalence des lignes d'abattage*, technical note, March.

1982b, *Manipulation et logement du bétail à l'abattoir*, study no. 9, November.

Chaudieu, G., 1965, *Boucher, qui es-tu? où vas-tu? ou la fabuleuse histoire des bouchers, celle d'hier, d'aujourd'hui et de demain*, followed by *Mémorial*, Paris (Peyronnet).

1970, *Le petit dictionnaire de boucherie et de boucherie-charcuterie*, Preface by Marcel Jouhandeau, Paris (Peyronnet).

1975, *Manuel pratique du boucher moderne et des techniques nouvelles*, seventh edition [first edition 1947], Paris (Dunod).

1980, *De la gigue d'ours au hamburger, ou la curieuse histoire de la viande*, Chennevières (La Corpo), 1980.

Chiva, M., 1979, 'Comment la personne se construit en mangeant', in *Communications* 31, November, pp. 107–18.

Corbin, A., 1982, *Les Filles de noce; misère sexuelle et prostitution (XIXe siècle)*, second edition [first edition Paris (Aubier-Montaigne), 1978], Paris (Flammarion).

1981, Introduction to A. Parent-Duchâtelet, *La Prostitution à Paris au XIXe siècle*, Paris (Le Seuil).

1982, *Le Miasme et la jonquille: L'odorat et l'imaginaire social, XVIII–XIXe siècles*, Paris (Aubier-Montaigne).

1984, 'Généalogie des pratiques', in *Déchets*, Paris (Centre Georges Pompidou), pp. 132–6.

Creswell, R. and Godelier, G. (eds.), 1976, *Outils d'enquête et d'analyse anthropologiques*, Paris (Maspéro).

Delarue, J., 1979, *Le Métier de bourreau*, Paris (Fayard).

Deterville, P., 1982, *Technologie de la viande*, fourth edition, Paris (Casteilla).

Détienne, M. and Vernant, J.-P., 1979, *La Cuisine du sacrifice en pays grec*, with contributions by J.-L. Durand, S. Georgoudi, F. Hartog and J. Svenbro, Paris (Gallimard).

Devereux, Georges [1970], 1977, *Essais d'ethnopsychiatrie générale*, third edition, Paris (Gallimard).

Douglas, M., 1967, *Purity and Danger*, London (Routledge).

Durand, J.-L., 1977, 'Le corps du délit', in *Communications* 26, pp. 46–61.

Elias, N., 1939, *Über den Prozess der Zivilisation*, vol. 1.

Fabre-Vassas, C., 1982, 'Le partage du ferum: un rite de chasse au sanglier', in *Etudes rurales* 87–8, July–December, pp. 377–400.

Farge, A., 1979a, *Vivre dans le rue à Paris au XVIIIe siècle*, Paris (Gallimard/Julliard).

1979b, 'Signe de vie, risque de mort. Essai sur le sang et la ville au XVIIIe siècle', in *Urbi* II, December, pp. XV–XXII.

Fossat, J.-L., 1971, *La formation du vocabulaire gascon de la boucherie et de la charcuterie. Etude de lexicologie historique et descriptive*, Toulouse (Ménard).

Gascar, Pierre, 1953, *Les Bêtes*, Paris (Gallimard).

1973, *Les bouchers*, Preface by G. Chaudieu, Paris (Delpire).

Genevoix, M., 1969, *Tendre bestiaire*, Paris (Plon).

Gomez da Silva, J.-C., 1983, 'Nous-mêmes, nous autres' in *L'Homme* XXIII, 3, July–September, pp. 55–80.

1984, 'Versants de la pollution', in *L'Homme* XXIV, 3–4, July-December, pp. 115–29.

Gonzalez-Crussi, F., 1984, *Notes of an Anatomist*, New York (Harcourt Brace).

Goubert, J.-P., 1986, *La conquête de l'eau; l'avènement de la santé à l'age industriel*, Paris (Laffont).

Guerrand, R.-H., 1985, *Les Lieux. Histoire des commodités*, Paris (La Découverte).

Héritier, Françoise, 1979a, 'Symbolique de l'inceste et de sa prohibition', in M. Izard and P. Smith (eds.), *La Fonction symbolique: essais d'anthropologie*, Paris (Gallimard), pp. 209–43.

1979b, 'Le Sang du guerrier et le sang des femmes. Notes anthropologiques sur le rapport des sexes', in *L'Africaine, Sexes et signes, Cahiers du GRIF* 29, winter 1984–5, pp. 7–21.

1981, *L'Exercice de la parenté*, Paris (EHESS/Gallimard/Le Seuil).

1985a, 'La Leçon des "primitifs"', in *L'Identité française*, Paris (Tierce), pp. 56–65.

1985b, 'Le Sperme et le sang. De quelques théories anciennes sur leur genèse et leurs rapports', in *Nouvelle revue de psychanalyse* 32, autumn, pp. 111–22.

Jamin, J., 1979 *La Tenderie aux grives chez les Ardennais du plateau*, Paris (Institut d'ethnologie du Musée de l'Homme).

Kuper, Jessica, (ed.), 1977, *The Anthropologists' Cookbook*, London.
1981, *La Cuisine des ethnologues* (translated from English), Paris (Berger Levrault).
Leach, Edmund, 1964, 'Anthropological Aspects of Language: Animal Categories and Verbal Abuse', in E. H. Lenneberg (ed.), *New Directions in the Study of Language*, Cambridge, Mass. (MIT Press).
Lebigre, A., 1979, 'La grande boucherie (XIIe–XIXe siècles)', in *L'Histoire* 17, November, pp. 41–9.
Legendre, P., 1978, 'La Différence entre nous', in *Critique* 375–6, August–September, pp. 848–63.
Le Goff, J., 1977, *Pour au autre Moyen-Age, Temps, travail et culture en Occident: 18 essais*, Paris (Gallimard).
Leguay, J.-P., 1984, *La Rue au Moyen-Age*, Rennes (Ouest-France).
Leroi-Gourhan, A. [1943], 1971, *L'homme et la matière*, vol. 1 of *Evolution et techniques*, second edition [first edition 1943], Paris (Albin Michel).
Léry, F., 1971, *Les Conserves*, third edition, Paris (PUF).
Lévi-Strauss, Claude, 1955, *Tristes Tropiques*, Paris (Plon).
1971, *Mythologiques, IV: L'Homme nu*, Paris (Plon).
1983, *Le Regard éloigné*, Paris (Plon).
Lister, M., [1698], 1986, 'The food and drink scene in Paris' [chapter entitled 'Of the food of Parisians' in *A Journey to Paris in the Year 1698*], in *Petits Propos culinaires* 22, London (Prospect Books), March, pp. 33–57.
Lizet, B., 1975, 'La Relation homme-cheval', in *L'Homme et l'animal, Actes du premier colloque d'ethnozoologie*, Paris (Institute international d'ethnosciences), pp. 341–9.
1982, *Le Cheval dans la vie quotidienne. Techniques et représentations du cheval de travail dans l'Europe industrielle*, Paris (Berger-Levrault).
Loux, F. and Richard, P., 1978, *Sagesse du corps. La santé et la maladie dans les proverbes françaises*, Paris (Maisonneuve et Larose).
Maertens, J.-T., 1978a, *Ritologiques 1; Le Dessein sur la peau. Essai d'anthropololgie des inscriptions tégumentaires*, Paris (Aubier-Montaigne).
1978b, *Ritologiques 4; Dans la peau des autres. Essai d'anthropologie des inscriptions vestimentaires*, Paris (Aubier-Montaigne).
Mèchin, C., 1983, 'Ethnologie d'une société forestière. Le boeuf d'attelage dans la vallée de la Plaine (Vosges)', in *Ethnozootechnie* no. 32, pp. 94–105.
Mercier, L.-S., [1781–8], 1982, *Le Tableau de Paris*, intr. and selec. by J. Kaplow, Paris (Maspéro).
Messiant, J., 1983, *Traditions culinaires de l'Houtland*, Hazebrouck (published by the author).
Miller, A. R., 1962, 'Slaughterhouse or abattoir', in *Encyclopaedia britannica*, vol. 20, pp. 771–3, Chicago/London/Toronto/Geneva (William Benton).
Parent-Duchâtelet, A., [1836], 1981, *La Prostitution à Paris au XIXe siècle* [1836], introduced and annoted by A. Corbin, Paris (Le Seuil).
Pélosse, V., 1981–2, 'Imaginaire social et protection de l'animal: des amis des bêtes de l'an X au législateur de 1850', in *L'Homme* XXII, 1, January–March, pp. 33–51.
Perrot, P., 1984, *Le Travail des apparences, ou les transformations du corps féminin XVIIIe–XIXe siècles*, Paris (Le Seuil).
Pingaud, Marie-Claude, 1978, *Paysans en Bourgogne: les gens de Minot*, Paris (Flammarion).
Pomiane, E. de, [1924], 1952, *Le Code de la bonne chère* [1924], Paris (Albin Michel).
Revel, J. [1979], 1982, *Un festin en paroles, Histoire littéraire de la sensibilité gastronomique de l'Antiquité à nos jours*, second edition [first edition Paris (Pauvert), 1979], Paris (Hachette).
Roger, A., 1978, *Nus et paysages, Essai sur la fonction de l'art*, Paris (Aubier).

Salvetti, F., 1980, *Le Boucher*, Paris (Berger-Levrault).
Sébillot, P., [1894], 1981, *Légendes et curiosités des métiers*, reprinted [first edition Paris (Flammarion), 1894–5] Marseille (Laffitte Reprints).
[1904] 1984, *Le Folklore de France, La Faune* [1904], Preface by Robert Delort, Paris (Imago).
Serres, 1985, *Les cinq sens: Philosophie des corps mêlés*, 1, Paris (Grasset).
Siesby, B., 1980, 'Blood is food', in *Petits Propos culinaires* 4, London (Prospect Books), February, pp. 41–9.
Sinclair, Upton, [1906], 1974, *The Jungle* [1906], reprinted Harmondsworth (Penguin).
Tabet, P., 1979, 'Les Mains, les outils, les armes', in *L'Homme* 29, 3–4, July–December, pp. 5–61.
Testard, A., 1986, *Essai sur les fondements de la division sexuelle du travail chez les chasseurs-cueilleurs*, Paris (E.H.E.S.S.).
Thomas, K., 1983, *Man and the Natural World: Changing Attitudes in England, 1500–1800*, Harmondsworth (Penguin).
Van Gennep, A., [1909], 1981, *Les Rites de passage* [1909, expanded edition 1969], reprinted Paris (Picard).
Verdier, Y., 1979, *Façons de dire, façons de faire, La Laveuse, la couturière, la cuisinière*, Paris (Gallimard).
Vialles, Noëlie, 1984, *Un 'terrain' didactique: L'Abattoir intercommunal du district Biarritz-Anglet-Bayonne*, diploma work for advanced studies in social anthropology, E.H.E.S.S., September, typescript.
Vigarello, G., 1985, *Le Propre et le sale, L'Hygiène du corps depuis le Moyen-Age*, Paris (Le Seuil).
Zimmermann, F., 1982, *La Jungle et le fumet des viandes: un thème écologique dans la médecine hindoue*, Paris (Hautes Etudes/Gallimard/Le Seuil).

INDEX

Page numbers in italic type refer to the figure/illustration on that page

CPSIA information can be obtained at www.ICGtesting.com
Printed in the USA
BVOW05s0029081214

378055BV00001B/11/P